RV OOPSIES
101 Dumb Things That RVers Do!

Larry MacDonald, Ph.D.

Copyright 2019 by MSI Press, LLC

All rights reserved. No part of this book may be reproduced or utilized in any form or by any means, electronic or mechanical, including photocopying, recording, or by any information storage and retrieval system, without permission in writing from the publisher.

For information, contact
MSI Press
1760-F Airline Highway, #203
Hollister, CA 95023

Photos

Cover Art: Robert McMahon

LCCN: 2019900020

ISBN: 978-1-942891-72-7

Dedication

To Danny and Julie and other RVers who are just starting out.

Larry MacDonald, Ph.D.

Contents

Dedication iii
Acknowledgements ix
INTRODUCTION 1
DUMB THINGS 5
    101. CURBSIDE MANNERS 7
    100. ROLLED MOLD 7
    99. STOP, LOOK, AND ASSESS THE MESS 8
    98. NO-PARKING GARAGE 8
    97. SIZE MATTERS 9
    96. OUT OF SIGHT, OUT OF MIND 9
    95. LOOK UP FOR HOOK UP 10
    94. HOLY CRAP 10
    93. TIGHT SQUEEZE 11
    92. IT'S THE SUDDEN STOP THAT HURTS 12
    91. UP ON THE ROOF 12
    90. WAIT FOR ME 13
    89. DIPS AND CHIPS 13
    88. A FULL-HOUSE FLUSH 14
    87. WHEN THE RUBBER HITS THE RIG 14
    86. BEST BEFORE DATE 15
    85. LIGHTS OUT 15
    84. MISSING AWNING 16
    83. A PLUMBER'S DELIGHT 17
    82. HASTE MAKES WASTE 17
    81. GIDDY-UP BIG FELLA 18
    80. THE IN'S AND OUT'S OF SLIDES 19
    79. RE-CAL-CU-LATING 19
    78. ROCKET MAN 20
    77. WINDY CITY 20
    76. UFO 22
    75. NO MORE DIRTY LAUNDRY 22
    74. SIDE-VIEW VISION 23
    73. WHERE'S THE KITTY 23
    72. RUNAWAY LUCKY 24
    71. FROZEN 25
    70. ADIOS AND HAVE A GOOD DAY 25
    69. ENJOY YOUR BISCUITS 26
    68. ALMOST HITCHED 27

- 67. BRAIN FREEZE 28
- 66. PINS AND DOLLYS 28
- 65. DON'T EVEN TRY TO THINK LIKE A MOUSE 29
- 64. MICE ARE NICE—OUTSIDE 29
- 63. LOOK BEFORE YOU LEAP 30
- 62. LET THERE BE LIGHT 31
- 61. DIESEL PUSHER 31
- 60. SEPARATION OF DUTIES 32
- 59. LIFE IS NOT A BEACH 32
- 58. BLACK AND BLUE TOAD 33
- 57. SEEING BLACK SPOTS 34
- 56. BUMPERS ARE FOR BUMPING 34
- 55. PITCH THE FORK 34
- 54. FRAYED BELTS LEAD TO FRAYED NERVES 35
- 53. BLACKWATER ON ICE 36
- 52. ON THE FLY 36
- 51. BLACKWATER SHOWER 37

DUMBER THINGS **39**
- 50. PARTING IS SUCH SORROW 41
- 49. TOW WOES 42
- 48. A REALLY HOT DAY IN DEATH VALLEY 42
- 47. JACKS ARE HIGH 43
- 46. SO-LOW 43
- 45. A FALLING APPLE 44
- 44. PATIENCE IS A VIRTUE 45
- 43. A SPOTTER IS ALSO A VIRTUE 45
- 42. RVING ON THE EDGE 46
- 41. YOU HAVE MAIL 47
- 40. HOLA SHOULDER 48
- 39. SWING YOUR PARTNER, NOT YOUR TAIL 48
- 38. POST TRAUMATIC SYNDROME 49
- 37. IT'S THE REAL THING 51
- 36. THE WHEEL GOES 'ROUND ... HOPEFULLY 52
- 35. PUMPS AND BUMPS 52
- 34. WHAT'S ON TV 53
- 33. IN THE HOT SEAT 53
- 32. I GO WHERE I'M TOWED TO ... USUALLY 53
- 31. BLUB, BLUB, BLUB 54
- 30. NASCAR IN THE REAR VIEW 55
- 29. Y BACK UP 55

- 28. MMM, MMM, NOT SO GOOD 56
- 27. BLACKWATER WOES 57
- 26. HIGHWAY TO HELL 57
- 25. WHERE'S THE REMOTE 58
- 24. BEACH-HEAD BOULEVARD 59
- 23. WELCOME TO PLEASANT VIEW 60
- 22. BLOWN WITH THE WIND 60
- 21. THINGS THAT GO BUMP IN THE NIGHT 61
- 20. SUCH A DEAL 62
- 19. A HURTFUL HOOKUP 62
- 18. CURBS, POSTS, AND MARTINIS 63
- 17. JUST DON'T BACK UP 64
- 16. HIJACKING 65
- 15. THERE'S A MUDDY ROAD AHEAD 65
- 14. THE CHAIN GANG 66
- 13. A HUMAN WHEEL-CHOCK 67
- 12. MR. SPARKY 67
- 11. FILL 'ER UP 68

DUMBEST THINGS..**69**
- 10. WHAT'S A DIPSTICK 71
- 9. A BATTERED TOAD 71
- 8. ALMOST CLEARING CUSTOMS 71
- 7. DOUBLE DUMB 73
- 6. THE NOSE KNOWS 73
- 4. WATER FALLS 75
- 3. ONE COOL TRIP 76
- 2. KEEP YOUR HEAD DOWN 77
- 1. SLIDES TRAVEL BEST WHEN RETRACTED 78

GENERAL OBSERVATIONS ABOUT RV MISHAPS................**81**
APPENDIX..**83**
About the Author **88**

Larry MacDonald, Ph.D.

Acknowledgements

First, I would like to thank all the RVers who shared their mishaps with me so that others can learn from their mistakes.

Second, I would like to thank Robert McMahon for the cover artwork, the three reviewers whose candid endorsements appear on the back cover, everyone who gave permission to use previously published text and photos, and the staff of MSI Press, especially Betty Lou Lever, Managing Editor, for their support in editing, publishing, and distributing this book.

And finally, I would like to thank my diligent co-pilot Sandy for ensuring (mostly) oops-free arrivals and departures from thousands of campgrounds during our 30-plus years of RVing together.

Larry MacDonald, Ph.D.

INTRODUCTION

"What's the dumbest thing you've done while RVing?" That's the question I've been asking fellow RVers over the past 10 years.

Every year, adventurous folks like us go camping in our RVs, and every year, we do some dumb things. Mostly, these are minor mishaps like running out of fuel or leaving something behind at a campsite, but sometimes they are major blunders, resulting in damage to our rigs. For the most part, RVers are a pretty smart bunch! Yet, mishaps do occur not only to newbies but to seasoned roadies as well. If you're one of us, you can probably think of at least one dumb thing that you wish you hadn't done while RVing. The good news, though, is that *all* of these mishaps can be avoided.

Each year, I selected ten mishaps reported to me, ranked them from Dumb to Dumbest, and published an article "RV Oops Awards" in several RV magazines in the US and Canada. This book presents 101 "awards," including some not previously published, and provides helpful hints on how they could have been avoided in the first place. Whether you camp in a motorhome, fifth-wheel, truck camper, trailer, or van, learning from the mistakes of others will help you avoid the same mistakes, making you a more competent and contented RVer.

Some helpful hints in this book have been deliberately repeated, such as

- always use a spotter; and
- always use a checklist.

Larry MacDonald, Ph.D.

If you learn nothing else from the 101 mishaps presented, doing just these two things will improve your chances of having an oops-free outing in your RV. Isn't that why you're reading this book—to have oops-free outings?

Let me begin with a confession: My wife, Sandy, and I have been RVing for over 30 years in various-sized motorhomes and fifth-wheel trailers. During that time—it hurts to say it—I've done a few dumb things, some more serious than others. My earliest oopsies involved departing campgrounds without checking the site and leaving behind various articles such as a doormat, dog toys, a tablecloth, a wheel chock, and probably some other things I still haven't been able to find! Doing so taught me a valuable lesson: Always check the site immediately after pulling out. I made up a Departure Checklist, which included "check site." Since then, I haven't left anything behind.

My second mishap involved hooking up our fifth-wheel trailer and pulling ahead without retracting the front jack stands. That was dumb! Replacing a bent jack stand was a tad more expensive than replacing a doormat and other stuff, but I learned two other valuable lessons:

- Don't be distracted by a neighboring camper who comes by in the middle of my departure routine to wish me a safe trip and chat about whatever!
- Always do a walk-around inspection *before* moving the rig!

My third major mishap is included among the 101 oopsies I describe in this book. For me, it was the costliest, but you won't be able to identify which one it is because all the RVers' names are fictitious. And I'm not giving an award for the sleuth who figures out which one it is! I've listed the mishaps as Dumb, Dumber, and Dumbest (in my opinion), saving the "Absolutely Dumbest," and likely the costliest, for last.

If you're an impatient sort like I am, you'll probably flip directly to the last page and read the Number 1 "Dumbest Thing" that someone reported to me while RVing. That's OK, but don't stop there. It's important that you read *all* of the oopsies so you won't repeat any of them and spoil an otherwise great outing. Not incidentally, you'll also save some grief and cash!

If you're an RVer planning to hit the road, you will definitely want to read this book so you don't actually "hit the road" as Robert and Roger did in Numbers 89 and 56. And if you're that impatient sort, you're probably ready to flip to Numbers 89 and 56! But don't! You'll get more out of this book by reading the mishaps sequentially as information about one oopsie sometimes leads to the next and so on. As I mention throughout, "Patience is a virtue."

Larry MacDonald, Ph.D.

DUMB THINGS

Larry MacDonald, Ph.D.

101. CURBSIDE MANNERS

Walt was parking his Class A motorhome alongside the curb in a small town. Unfortunately, the sloping street tilted the top of his unit toward the sidewalk, enough to rub against a metal street sign. **OOPS!** A four-foot scratch on the side did not quite match the swirled paint job.

Walt sat on the roof and pushed the offending sign away with his feet while his wife edged their motorhome forward until it cleared the sign. He later visited a body shop that made it look new again. Walt commented, "I am now super-cautious about street signs when parking curbside. Never again!"

Helpful hint: Although it never happened again to Walt, that same mishap was reported to me by several other RVers so pay close attention to signs when maneuvering close to a curb.

100. ROLLED MOLD

It was raining on Herb's last day of camping in the fall. He rolled up the wet awning and left it that way until his first camping trip in the spring. When he unrolled it, he discovered exotic fungi that thrive in dark, damp conditions had transformed the blue-and-white fabric into earthy shades of black and green.

Herb's short-term solution was simple but tedious: scrub for hours with detergent, trying not to look up when cleaning the underside. His long-term solution was to make sure that his wet awning is opened and dried before storing it for an extended period.

Helpful hint: If you have an older rig and find yourself taking a shower while cleaning the underside of your awning, try detaching the two support bars at the bottom and allow them to slide under the unit until the awning is more like a wall than a ceiling. This two-person procedure may require some bracing in order to apply pressure on your scrub brush.

99. STOP, LOOK, AND ASSESS THE MESS

Steve was backing his Class C motorhome into a campsite with his wife in the passenger seat. He heard shouts coming from an adjacent campsite and stopped to see what all the commotion was about. He had backed over a small cedar tree, which was lodged at a rakish angle under the rear quarter section. In his haste to extricate his rig from the tree, Steve pulled forward. **RIPPPP!** The partially uprooted tree ripped off the lower side and rear aluminum panels.

After sheepishly replanting the tree, Steve used a handful of metal screws to temporarily reattach the RV panels. His final fix involved a pricey visit to the body shop. Since the mishap, Steve always ensures that his wife is watching behind the rig to give directions when he backs up. He even purchased a set of headphones so they can communicate without shouting or arm waving.

> **Helpful hint:** If your rig ever gets entangled in tree branches, always stop and assess whether less damage will occur by judiciously cutting off branches rather than simply pulling away and hoping for the best.

98. NO-PARKING GARAGE

Randy was driving his Class C into a shopping center lot on a rainy day and chose to enter the underground parking area. His rig fit easily into the entrance, but unknown to him, the farther he proceeded into the darkened lot, the lower the ceiling became. **CRUNCH!** His air-cooling unit wedged itself tightly under a concrete beam.

Randy managed to back out, but the casing of the cooling unit was smashed beyond repair and water was leaking inside the rig. His less-than-satisfactory solution was to remove the cooling unit and replace it with a carrying case large enough to cover the hole. Randy now shies away from underground parking regardless of how hard it's raining.

> **Helpful hint:** It's important to know the height of your rig, plus allow a comfortable margin for error, and to constantly be aware of overhead obstacles such as entranceways, wires, and branches. Even the horizontal "Height Pipes" suspended at the entrances to some parking lots can cause damage if they come into contact with your vehicle.

97. SIZE MATTERS

Brian bought a fifth-wheel trailer and had a hitch installed in his short-bed pickup. Everything worked fine until he made his first sharp turn. **KA-BOOM!** The front corner of his trailer hit the truck's back window, shattering it to smithereens. Fortunately, no one was injured, including his dog in the back seat. Surprisingly, Brian said the hitch installer never mentioned the potential problem of the trailer contacting the truck when turning.

Brian's temporary solution was to duct-tape a sheet of plastic to the window frame. He also slid the hitch farther back in his truck bed, which may have created another unsafe condition by taking weight off the front wheels used for steering and braking. His ultimate solution, after replacing the window, was to buy a long-bed pickup.

> **Helpful hint:** Although a long-bed pickup is ideal for a fifth-wheel trailer, a less-expensive option would have been to install a kingpin extender or a hitch specifically designed for short-bed pickups.

96. OUT OF SIGHT, OUT OF MIND

Occasionally, you'll see an RV traveling down the highway with the TV antenna raised. Those are the lucky ones. Grant never made it to the highway. His raised antenna hit a tree limb while exiting the campground. **WACK!** Fortunately, he was able to find repair parts at a local RV dealer, where the clerk made him feel better by saying, "It happens all the time."

Grant said he solved the problem of forgetting to lower his antenna by "attaching a long piece of velvet material from the crank handle when the antenna is raised." For later models that raise and lower antennae electrically, a long piece of velvet material could be attached beside the switch as a reminder. Personally, I would put "Lower Antenna" on my Departure Checklist, and then attach a long piece of velvet material beside the Checklist as a reminder to use it!

95. LOOK UP FOR HOOK UP

Power cords are plugged in upon arrival at a campground and unplugged prior to departure. That's what I thought until Charlie told me about the time he departed a campsite in his Class C after doing a walkaround inspection. A hesitation in forward movement was followed by a noise from the rear of his rig. **TWANG!** In his rearview mirror, he saw the power pole quivering back and forth. Upon inspection, Charlie was reminded that the power outlet on this pole was elevated five feet above the ground. He had suspended the cord on his RV ladder and actually walked under it during his walk around.

Since that incident, Charlie always walks around his motorhome twice, once looking down and once again looking up, vowing never again to forget to unplug his power cord.

Many RVers admit to driving down the road with a trailing power cord, which is usually damaged beyond repair from dragging on the pavement. Charlie at least had a reasonable excuse for forgetting to unplug. For electrical connections at ground level, forgetting to do a walkaround is a costly excuse.

94. HOLY CRAP

Bill and Jane had just finished dressing for church and had about a half-hour before leaving. While Jane continued putting on her makeup, Bill noticed his blackwater tank was 3/4 full and decided to use the time to empty it. He pulled the blackwater valve and let it drain. Since he still had some time left, he decided to rinse out all the paper and sewage in the top quarter of the tank by filling it completely, which he estimated would take about 12 minutes.

At the 12-minute mark, the "full" indicator light was not yet "on," so he yelled to his wife to check the water level in the toilet. She obliged by pushing the button that electrically opens the flap valve. **WHOOSH!** A brown geyser, complete with little pieces of toilet paper and fecal matter, covered her hair, face, and clothing as well as the bathroom walls, ceiling, and floors. As the screaming waned, Bill shut off the water and drained the tank while Jane jumped in the shower. Bill cleaned up the mess as best he could, and they still made it to church, though a bit late.

In his sermon about taking God and spouses for granted, the pastor remarked that everyone should regularly "fertilize their relationship with God and their spouse." Bill, biting his tongue to keep from laughing out loud, leaned over and whispered to Jane, "I fertilized you this morning." She hit him!

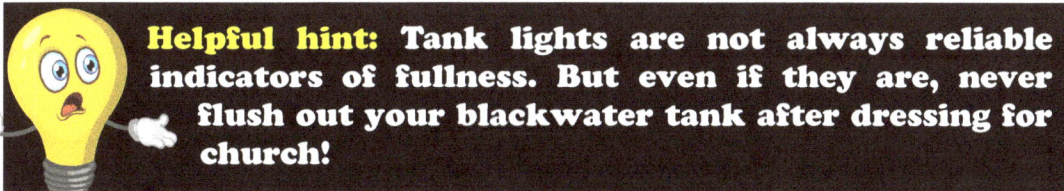

Helpful hint: Tank lights are not always reliable indicators of fullness. But even if they are, never flush out your blackwater tank after dressing for church!

93. TIGHT SQUEEZE

On a cross-Canada trip in their Class C, Don approached a bridge with a tollbooth. He drove ahead slowly, ensuring that the RV height did not exceed the gate overhead and that the side mirrors did not exceed the entrance width. As he entered the payment area, **CRUNCH!** "What the heck was that?" Backing out, he discovered that a 3-foot-high cement wall just below the passenger-side mirror had ripped off the front bracket of his awning. Moving over to an unused lane, Don duct-taped the bracket in place, which allowed him to proceed to a dealership for a proper repair.

Don now has a new rule, which all RVers should adopt when passing through tollgates: "Always use the lanes intended for semi-trailers."

Incidentally, another RVer pulling a trailer reported exactly the same mishap at the same tollbooth in Nova Scotia. Based on the number of collisions with this concrete wall, one would think the authorities would move it back a foot or so, or at least put up a sign: RVs USE TRUCK LANE.

92. IT'S THE SUDDEN STOP THAT HURTS

Most RVers take pride in the appearance of their rigs, ensuring that they are washed and waxed on a regular basis. Of course, doing so usually involves the use of a ladder to reach the upper areas. Be careful, very careful when using a ladder.

After a long trip south for the winter, Ross's motorhome needed some serious cleaning. He got out his 7-foot folding ladder and climbed up to the next-to-top rung to wash above the windshield. Suddenly, the ladder began to fold underneath him. He watched helplessly as the pavement rushed up to stop his fall. Ross lay there wondering how badly he was hurt while his neighbors rushed over to help, calling an ambulance, and making sure he didn't try to get up. X-rays at the hospital showed multiple broken bones: arm, pelvis, shoulder, and ribs.

During his lengthy recovery, Ross had lots of time to think about what went wrong, confirmed by examining his ladder's remains: he had neglected to lock the four legs of the ladder. Fortunately, Ross sufficiently recovered to again wash his motorhome—"but only if someone holds the ladder!"

> **Helpful hints:** Make sure your ladder is locked and has a secure footing. Never stand on the top two rungs: the higher you go on a ladder, the more it hurts when you fall. A long-handle brush can be used to clean the upper portions of your rig. If you have balance problems, consider hiring someone to do the work.

91. UP ON THE ROOF

Alan decided it was time to clean the roof of his motorhome while it was parked in the driveway. Since his model did not have an attached ladder, he propped his extension ladder against the side and climbed up with a hose and cleaning supplies. While spraying down the roof, his hose caught the ladder and knocked it down. **OOPS!**

Alan's wife was not due home for another four hours, but quite a few cars were passing by in view of the rig. He figured he would just wave and someone would stop to help. For more than an hour, he waved. The few motorists who noticed him waved back and kept on driving. Finally, a man stopped and put the ladder back up. Alan sheepishly thanked him and decided to clean his roof another day.

When Alan reported this mishap to me, he still hadn't figured out how to prevent a reoccurrence. I suggested several options:

- use a distress wave (crisscrossing arms above the head) rather than a friendly "Hi, there" wave;
- carry a cellphone aloft to call for help;
- tie a rope to the ladder and secure the other end topside; or
- clean the roof for four hours until his wife got home.

90. WAIT FOR ME

Tim and his family were returning home on the freeway after a camping trip when traffic came to a standstill, the result of an accident. During the next hour, each family member passed the time in his or her own way: Tim read a book; his wife took the dog for a walk; their daughter did homework. When traffic finally began to move, the dog was curled up in the front seat, and Tim assumed his wife was taking a nap in the back. Fortunately, before getting up to speed, he glanced in the passenger-side mirror and saw his wife, running along the shoulder, yelling, and waving her arms (hopefully, in a crisscross fashion above her head!). Tim quickly stopped the coach, allowing her to catch up and come aboard, totally out of breath. She had gone for another walk—without the dog.

Tim has since expanded his Departure Checklist: Antenna lowered? Steps raised? Wife aboard?

89. DIPS AND CHIPS

During his family's first cross-country trip in their new Class C, Robert was taking no chances of doing anything stupid that might qualify for an RV Oops Award. He always used checklists and even left himself notes to check his checklists. Partway through their journey, Robert noted it was time for an oil change and proceeded to drive from the road to the parking lot of a lube shop. Noticing a distinct dip in the curb, he decided to reduce sway by lining up for a direct-in approach. Bad decision!

As the front end leveled off and the rear wheels approached the dip, he heard a loud, horrid scraping sound and immediately lost forward motion. The trailer hitch had gotten stuck on the road, suspending the rear wheels over the dip. Fortunately, the lube crew assisted by jacking up the rear end and placing boards under the wheels, allowing Robert to continue into the shop for his oil change.

When exiting, Robert chose a more angular track through the dip. The only damage was to the wiring harness on the hitch and to his pride (his kids were "laughing hysterically"). I suggested to Robert that he might want to add dips to one of his checklists.

88. A FULL-HOUSE FLUSH

After a week of camping in his brand-new motorhome, Rick decided to use his blackwater-tank cleanout sprayer for the very first time. Following the directions in his operator's manual, he pulled the valve handle to "Ensure the blackwater valve is open." He then hooked up the water hose to the appropriate tank-flush intake and turned on the faucet. About ten minutes later, his wife began yelling frantically from inside: "Rick! Come quickly! Toilet water is running all over the carpets!" It was also running out of the vent pipe on the roof. **OOPS!**

Rick's mistake was simple but troublesome: he had opened the graywater valve instead of the black. He quickly shut off the faucet, opened the blackwater valve, and spent the next few hours cleaning carpets and washing down the outside. His now-used motorhome was almost like new again, except for the lingering smell of disinfectant.

> **Helpful hint:** Since some RV manufacturers haven't seen fit to install gray handles on graywater valves, consider painting those handles gray and leaving your blackwater handle black.

87. WHEN THE RUBBER HITS THE RIG

Gary was driving his older Class C along a freeway when he heard a loud BOOM, sounding like a cannon firing in the back of his rig. Pulling over,

RV OOPSIES

he found that one rear tire had exploded, throwing a large chunk of rubber through the wheel well, tearing out an interior cabinet, and making a major mess of the bathroom. Gary seldom checked the tires, but hindsight suggested he should have.

He limped to the closest tire store where he purchased six new tires. He later visited a body shop and cabinetmaker to repair the internal damage. Gary's walkaround now includes a close inspection of all tires for proper inflation, cracks, and wear, and as we'll see in the following mishap, the age of the tires regardless of condition.

86. BEST BEFORE DATE

Alf was driving his Class A along a freeway when he heard a loud **BOOM**, coming from the back of his coach (similar to what Gary heard!). Pulling over, he found that one rear tire had exploded, throwing a chunk of rubber through the wheel well, damaging an interior cabinet. With his flashers on, he drove slowly to the nearest tire shop, where the salesman recommended, he replace all six tires. "Why all six? The tread is like new?" Alf asked.

"Because they are ten years old. Most tire manufacturers recommend changing them after six or seven years, regardless of tread wear."

Alf occasionally checked his tires for inflation, cracks, and tread wear but never for age. He assumed that by using his motorhome only during the summer months, his tires should last longer. Not so, he learned from the salesman, "Tires that sit for extended periods, especially on damp ground and in direct sunlight, deteriorate more quickly than those used regularly."

> **Helpful hints:** A tire's age can be determined by the last 4 digits of the DOT code, for example: 4216. The first two digits refer to the week of manufacture, and the last two digits refer to the year, in this case, the 42nd week of 2016. If your rig is going to be parked for an extended period, always drive onto boards, and attach fitted covers over your tires.

85. LIGHTS OUT

Bert had just arrived at a campground and hooked up his hoses and cables as he had done many, many times before. After dinner, he and his wife sat down to watch TV. About an hour into their favorite program, the lights and TV flickered on and off for several minutes, then turned off completely. Assuming the power went off in the campground, they went to bed early. The next morning, after reporting their power outage to the office, a maintenance staff came by to check it out. **OOPS!**

Bert's 50-amp plug was only pushed in halfway, causing arcing within the receptacle. The plastic receptacle was partially melted, and one of the three prongs had completely burned off, requiring the purchase of a new cord. Bert said, "From now on, I will always push in my power cord completely."

After reading this, I suspect you will too. In fact, I think about this incident every time I connect my power cord.

84. MISSING AWNING

On the last day of his camping trip, Ben rolled up the awning and hit the road. Unfortunately, he neglected to secure it with the locking latches on each of the two support bars. It pretty much stayed in place until he got up to cruising speed. **KABOOM!**

The wind had unrolled the awning, tearing the worn canvas and ripping the support bars from their attachment points on the side of his coach. Ben rolled up the mess as best he could, using rope to hold the dangling bars against the side. He then drove slowly home, where he permanently removed the damaged awning. I asked Ben, "Do you miss your awning?" He replied, "Only when it's rainy or sunny."

83. A PLUMBER'S DELIGHT

Jay, a long-time tent camper, made the big decision to buy a small motorhome and take his family camping in style. Shortly after hooking up his freshwater line, water started running from underneath onto the ground. A line had burst under the kitchen sink. After shutting off the water, he used tape to repair the line. Within a few minutes after turning on the water, he saw another leak under the bathroom sink, which only required a crimp, and another leak behind the toilet. More tape.

He immediately called the RV dealer, who told him to check his pressure regulator. "My what?" Jay asked.

Following the dealer's explanation, he purchased and installed a regulator. He has had no further problems with leaks.

> **Helpful hints:** To prevent bursting water lines, always use a pressure regulator at the outlet of the campground's water tap which is factory preset around 50 pounds per square inch (PSI) of water pressure. RV plumbing, especially on older models, and filters are not designed for the high-pressure water lines found at some campgrounds. Most RV outlets also sell a pressure-regulator gauge, which indicates the PSI and can be adjusted to your manufacturer's recommended maximum pressure, sometimes closer to 60 PSI or higher.

82. HASTE MAKES WASTE

Dave's first priority, after maneuvering his large Class A into a smallish campsite, was to dump his full blackwater tank. His sewer hose was just a couple of inches too short. Since it was raining, Dave decided not to take time to attach his extension hose. Instead, he gained the required length by attaching a 45-degree connector parallel to the ground and stretching his hose to the maximum. Immediately after pulling the tank-valve handle, the weight of liquid pulled down on the hose, unscrewing the connector from the discharge pipe. **OOPS!**

Five days of excrement began pouring out onto the ground. In his haste to shut off the flow, Dave broke the valve handle. Rather than fill his campsite with raw sewage, he chose to reattach the hose, an unpleasant task considering what was spewing into his lap at 10 gallons per minute. He eventually succeeded and held onto the connector until the tank was empty.

Dave then visited the campground's washroom for an extralong shower, clothes and all. He decided to throw his shoes away! In retrospect, I'm guessing Dave would have preferred getting wet from rainwater rather than from blackwater.

> **Helpful hint:** Remember the rule: "Right is tight, left is loose." Screws, nuts, light bulbs, and sewer-hose connectors all tighten to the right (clockwise) and loosen to the left (counterclockwise). Thus, if your 45-degree hose connector is pointed right, a downward force will tighten it. Dave's connector was likely pointing left, primed to loosen by the weight of the discharge liquid.

81. GIDDY-UP BIG FELLA

Jerry was driving his brand new 45-foot motorhome on a four-lane divided highway when he became desperate for a restroom break.

The nearest rest area was just ahead on the left-hand side, which required him to pass across two oncoming lanes to enter. He pulled into the turn lane and waited patiently. After a minute or two, he saw oncoming traffic but figured he had time to make it before they got to him. As Jerry described it, "In that moment, my brain thought I was in a sports car, not a 50,000-pound motorhome. So, I floored the gas pedal to get across before the traffic." As he pulled into the lot at an excessive rate of speed, he heard a giant **THUMP** caused by the frontend grounding out.

After parking, he got out to look. "My heart sank, and I literally felt sick. I completely forgot I had to use the restroom!"

The force of the impact had ripped loose the top end of the generator cap (a 3-foot-by-3-foot piece of fiberglass) so it was hanging out at a 45-degree angle from the front of the coach. Using some Gorilla Tape, he temporarily reattached the fiberglass cap back to the front of the coach ("It looked really classy, as you can imagine!"). Later, with a fiberglass repair kit from an auto part's store, Jerry was able to fix it, "except for some scratches on the bottom that serve as a reminder not to drive my motorhome the same way I would a Porsche."

Helpful hint: Patience is a virtue that also pays dividends. Sometimes, taking an extra few minutes when in traffic or to peruse a Checklist can prevent a bruised ego and a damaged rig.

80. THE IN'S AND OUT'S OF SLIDES

John and Trish were preparing to depart a campground in their Class A. John had opened a panel to unhook the water hose and left it open. Awhile later, he went inside to close a slide, checking carefully to ensure there wasn't anything in the way. Trish was busy putting dishes away and securing drawers so no one was outside to watch the slide come in. It was nearly in when a loud **CRUNCH** was followed by the slide abruptly stopping.

A look outside showed the open panel door was badly bent by the slide and the slide itself skewed at an angle. By opening and closing the slide several times, the angle became less until the slide again came in straight. The panel door didn't fare as well and had to be replaced.

Helpful hint: Always ensure that someone is inside and someone outside when operating slides. Things sometimes get crunched inside as well as outside when opening and closing these huge compartments.

79. RE-CAL-CU-LATING

The use of a GPS to find campgrounds, gas stations, and other locations has made life easier for RVers. Well, sometimes! My friend Anne was taking her first cross-country trip in her Class C and purchased a GPS to make life easier. I suggested to her that she always use a map to confirm the route recommended by the GPS. She obviously ignored this advice when trying to get to a campground and "Old Faithful" told her to turn right at an intersection.

A rural road with a slight upgrade soon became steep and winding with overhanging trees on the left and a cliff on the right, forcing Anne to ride the center. The 30-mile road dead-ended at a seldom-visited fort. **OOPS!** She then had to backtrack (a total of 60 nerve-wracking miles) to the intersection where turning left would have taken her almost immediately to the campground.

Anne confessed that she didn't use a map to confirm her route, adding some words of wisdom: "Eating humble pie is low in calories but high in humility."

78. ROCKET MAN

The manager of the storage lot where Bruce parked his Class A phoned to tell him that a rock thrown from a lawnmower had broken his door window. The window was replaced, courtesy of the manager. To prevent a reoccurrence, Bruce decided to drape a towel over the top of the door and down the outside, covering the window. To do this, he stood on the steps facing outward with the door open in front of him and the partially open screen door behind him. As he was swinging the towel over, he accidentally backed into the screen door and the steps retracted. The electric switch was positioned in the mode, which retracted the steps if either door was closed.

Here is Bruce's description of the event in his own words: "The steps were fast, really fast, clamping the back of my running shoes and sending me flying out onto the driveway. My feet came out of the shoes, and I ended up horizontal on the gravel with a twisted knee and ankle. Robin Williams would have been proud of me."

Helpful hint: If you're going to be standing on the steps of your motorhome with the door open, make sure the retract switch is in the Off position.

77. WINDY CITY

This incident was the first time there were multiple winners for an RV Oops Award. Fortunately, I was there to take notes and photos.

Near Palm Springs, California, a serious windstorm with blowing sand arrived in mid-afternoon, knocking down a few trees, and generally causing havoc in the campground. As a precaution when the wind picked up, I closed my windows and hatches and pulled in the slides. After the wind subsided, I went outside to assess damages. Our doormat had blown onto the roadway. Other campers were less fortunate.

One fellow was inspecting his vinyl slide canopy, which had ripped away from the side of his coach and was merrily flapping in the breeze. Another had his awning blown over the top of his rig, bending the support arms. Two other guys were searching downwind for a plastic roof vent, which had been left open, and a canvas wheel cover. A couple of satellite dishes were lying on their sides. A sewer hose had become dislodged from the drainpipe, resulting in gray water being spewed about the site (which the owner wasn't aware of until I told him).

Later, I spoke with a couple who had gone away and left their windows and hatches open. A substantial layer of sand had settled on every horizontal surface throughout their motorhome. I can imagine: Even with our windows, hatches, and slides closed, we were finding sand in nooks and crannies for days afterward.

 **Helpful hint:** It's always a good idea to keep an eye on the weather. If severe storms are forecast, secure everything outside and close your windows, hatches, and slides.

76. UFO

Mike was driving his coach on a busy freeway when a pickup truck loaded with various construction items passed and moved over in front of him. Within a mile or so, a large piece of plywood came flying out of the back of the truck and sailed up over the top of his motorhome. KABOOM!

Mike pulled over at the first opportunity to inspect the damage. The wood had mangled his satellite dish to the point where it had to be replaced. While costly, this accident could have been worse, much worse, if that sheet of plywood had come through the windshield.

> **Helpful hint:** Always be aware of vehicles in front of you carrying loads that appear to be unsecured. If you choose not to pass them, then slow down to allow sufficient stopping distance should something fall off or become airborne.

75. NO MORE DIRTY LAUNDRY

Jay and Wendy purchased a new motorhome in Canada with a fancy Italian-made washer/dryer combo, which worked fine during their first winter down south. After returning home, they stored their coach for six months. On their next trip south, the washer stopped working. A mobile RV technician diagnosed the problem as a faulty motor and replaced it under the warranty conditions, which did not cover the $65 service call.

After again storing their coach for six months back in Canada, they went south, and the washer quit again. Jay called the same mobile technician who again replaced the motor, still under warranty, and again charged for the service call. This time, he recommended that the washer be used regularly while in storage to lubricate the motor bearings. Wendy remarked, "I used this opportunity to do a monthly load of wash." They've had no further problems with the washer motor.

> **Helpful hint:** Appliances, and RVs in general, have fewer mechanical issues when used on a regular basis.

74. SIDE-VIEW VISION

Gordy was driving his Class A on a freeway, pulling a trailer loaded with an ATV, when the sky opened up with rain so heavy he could barely see the road. He put on the flashers and maneuvered to the side of the road to wait it out.

Just then, his wife looked at their rearview camera monitor and screamed in horror, "The trailer's gone!" The thought of a trailer sitting somewhere on the highway in a blinding storm panicked them both. Gordy immediately called 911 and explained that he had just lost a trailer on the Interstate. He was told that because of the storm, it would be some time before the police could assist them. The rain continued so hard that they stayed in the motorhome for another 15 minutes, all the time dreading the worst. When it finally let up, Gordy went back to check out the damage and found the trailer hooked to the motorhome just where it was supposed to be.

Admittedly puzzled, Gordy looked again at the camera monitor and noticed that the view was from the driver's-side camera, which was indeed looking back down the empty highway. By putting on the flashers, the functional camera had switched from the rear to the driver's side, just as it does when the left turn signal is used. Gordy called back 911 and told them that they had found the trailer. He hung up when the operator asked where they had found it!

73. WHERE'S THE KITTY

After buying groceries, Tom and Mary became preoccupied with transferring items from the shopping cart into their Class C motorhome at the far end of the parking lot. Once everything was securely stowed, Tom drove through the lot onto a busy street, turned at the first intersection, and pulled into a gas station a half-block down the street. While waiting in line at the pump, Mary noticed that their 20-year-old cat, "Bob" (how's that for an alias?), was not with them. Assuming that he must have escaped at their last stop, Tom grabbed a walkie-talkie and hurriedly jogged back to the grocery store. Meanwhile, Mary pulled their motorhome up to the pump, got out, and "couldn't believe my eyes when I noticed Bob near some bushes beside the gas station." After gathering him into her arms, she called Tom with the good news.

I'm still trying to visualize Bob frantically following his "home" as it meandered the quarter-mile from the store to the gas station: "Wait for me!"

Talk about cats having nine lives; this old guy definitely used up one on that occasion!

> **Helpful hint:** When traveling with pets, whenever a door or window has been opened, always ensure that they are on board before moving the rig. Most pets will find their way back to their home when they decide it's time (usually to eat). Only rarely, will they chase it down the highway!

72. RUNAWAY LUCKY

Arriving at a local campground, Bev parked her Class C in a pull-through site and unhitched the tow car, leaving it behind her motorhome. The next morning it was gone. She ran to neighboring campers in tears, shouting, "Somebody stole my car!" No one had seen or heard anything. Shortly thereafter, a friend arrived. After some hysterics from Bev about her loss, the friend said she thought she saw her car down at the entrance to the campground. They walked down the slight incline to the entrance and, sure enough, there was her car.

Bev had locked the doors but left the car in Neutral with the emergency brake off. Handprints on the dirty hood and side mirror suggested vandals had pushed the car backward out of the site onto the incline. From there, it proceeded across several tiers of campsites narrowly missing trees, picnic tables, and fire rings, eventually stopping when the frame got hung up on a large concrete block. The rear bumper had some serious scratches, and one rear tire was off the ground. The tow bill came to $150.

The dinghy, which she now calls "Lucky," is once again parked behind Bev's motorhome—locked and in gear, with the emergency brake on.

71. FROZEN

Bill and Sheila were fall camping in Montana with their granddaughter, who was enjoying the new-fallen snow. After a weekend of lowering temperatures, it was time to leave. Unfortunately, the support jacks of their older motorhome—two in the back and one centrally located in the front—were frozen to the ground. The motors labored, but the jacks weren't budging. Bill took a hatchet underneath and started chipping away at the ice covering the bases of the rear jacks. That seemed to work okay; both jacks retracted. So, he crawled under the front, between the jack and the wheel, and continued chipping. After several minutes, the jack base retracted, and the front axle came crashing down, pinning Bill underneath on his stomach.

Sheila came running out to see what had happened. Her suggestion was to start the engine and lower the jack, but Bill, slightly panicked, wasn't at all comfortable with that! Instead, he handed her the axe so she could start chipping away a trench below his legs, which were sticking out under the front bumper. Ten minutes later, with her pulling and him pushing, Bill wiggled his way along the trench until free. In hindsight, Bill agreed that starting the engine and lowering the jack might have worked, providing his wife made sure the transmission was in Park and the emergency brake was on. Sheila smiled.

Helpful hint: In cold weather, always lower leveling jacks onto dry boards rather than directly onto the ground to help prevent freezing and sinking.

70. ADIOS AND HAVE A GOOD DAY

Perry and his wife were spending a couple of weeks in Mexico camping in their motorhome. One day, they and another couple agreed to go shopping in a nearby town, using Perry's Class A motorhome since neither had a tow car. As often happens on outings, the guys sat up front with the gals in the back. After shopping, Perry was maneuvering his coach through the crowded parking lot while Chuck was showing off his new watch, talking about what a great deal he had made. In a tight turn, the right front corner of the motorhome clipped and broke off a truck mirror.

Seconds later, the owner of the truck was pounding on the door. After some frantic hand waving and shouting in Spanish, it was obvious he was not happy. Partly to calm him down, Perry immediately gave him $200 to replace the mirror. The man seemed satisfied, and Perry was relieved he didn't have to deal with the police or his insurance company.

Scratches on his motorhome continue to remind Perry to not get distracted while driving, especially while maneuvering in a crowded parking lot. Chuck also learned a lesson and apologized for talking about his shopping experience at exactly the wrong time.

69. ENJOY YOUR BISCUITS

This story was relayed to me by Ruth whose grandparents had decided they would buy a motorhome and "hit the road before they got much older." They purchased a new Class A and planned a trial run to several State campgrounds. After a couple of weeks at their first campground, it was time to move on to another not far away. While they were pulling in the slides and raising the jacks, a neighboring RVer came over and offered them a plate of biscuits for the next leg of their trip. How nice is that?

After thanking the neighbor and getting into the front seats, they drove out of the campsite. As they neared the exit, a fellow camper was waving his arms and pointing to the side of their coach. Their electrical cord, hose, and sewer line, which they had forgotten to detach, were all dragging along behind. **OOPS!** Annoyed and embarrassed, they finished their departure routine and carried on.

According to Ruth, her grandparents love the RV lifestyle, particularly the friendly campers they meet along the way. One thing they learned from the experience is to always do a walkaround before departing to ensure they really are ready to hit the road.

Helpful hint: While doing a walk around, instead of just looking, consider using a checklist, either written or on an iPhone or iPad, using an app such as RV CheckList. For your convenience, I made up an Arrival and a Departure Checklist for a Class C, which is included in the Appendix and can also be found on my website: http://www.landyachting.ca/tips/

68. ALMOST HITCHED

Joe was getting ready to depart the campground after a great weekend of waterskiing and fishing at the adjoining lake. His final task was to hook up his boat trailer to the hitch receiver on the back of his diesel pusher. While he was in the process of doing so, a friendly camper came over and asked, "Joe, where are you headed?" Being a sociable guy, Joe explained that they were off to another campground and another lake. Conversation continued as Joe walked to the front of his motorhome, said goodbye, and drove off.

When he reached the highway and got up to speed, he could hear a rattling noise at the rear of the coach. Pulling off to the side of the road, Joe applied his brakes purposely to stop in a hurry, resulting in a loud **CRUNCH!** An inspection showed the trailer had become disconnected from the coach and the hitch firmly implanted in the radiator, causing steam to shoot skyward.

Thinking back about his hook-up procedure, Joe recalled that his camping neighbor interrupted him just after he had attached the trailer and just before he normally tightened down the hitch clamp. That brief conversation resulted in a $2,000 repair bill and a vow to always use a checklist, especially when well-meaning neighbors interrupt his departure routine.

As the above two mishaps illustrate, RVers tend to be a sociable lot, always willing to lend a helping hand. We've all experienced the delight of nearby campers coming over to welcome us to the campground or wish us well upon departure. I refer to them as "Arrival or Departure Committees." As well-meaning as these cordial chats are, they can sometimes sidetrack us from our normal routines, leading to mishaps.

The key here, if you are the sociable type, is to wait until arriving or departing campers are completely finished with their duties before engaging them in conversation unless of course, it appears that they require assistance, such as needing a back-up spotter, lifting a heavy boat trailer, or trying to fix a defective whatever.

On the other hand, if you are the arriving or departing RVer engaged in a task, politely tell your new friend(s), "How about we chat later, as soon as I finish my routine?" You might have fewer friends, but you'll definitely have less grief and more cash!

67. BRAIN FREEZE

Robbie had just purchased a new car and towed it to a local campground. Not wanting to unhook his car, he chose a pull-through site. As his wife was making dinner, Robbie was admiring his new car from the driver's seat. Before going inside the coach, he moved the gearshift lever from Neutral to Park.

After dinner, his wife mentioned the coach was not quite level, and maybe they could back up a bit to try to level it. Robbie agreed, so he fired up the engine and slowly backed up. Within 2 feet he heard a **CRUNCH**. Getting out to investigate, he saw that the car had not moved, but the hitch had risen up to the point where it broke the panel under the front bumper. Six hundred dollars later, his new car was like new again. To this day, Robbie has no idea why he put the shift lever into Park (maybe he was thinking it should be in Park when they were parked?).

66. PINS AND DOLLYS

Henry and his wife had just arrived at a big-box-store parking lot in their Class A and wanted to do some shopping in a local downtown area. After unloading the car from their two-wheel dolly, off they went. Upon returning, Henry ran the car up onto the dolly and strapped down the front wheels. With several hours of daylight remaining, they decided to drive to a campground. While heading down a four-lane highway, Henry heard some scraping sounds but couldn't find a pullover to check it out. A passenger in a passing car was waving frantically at them from an open window while pointing to the rear of their motorhome, shouting: "**Sparks!**"

At the first opportunity Henry pulled over and walked back to his tow dolly. Everything seemed fine until he looked more closely at the dolly platform. The pin to prevent the ramp from lowering should have been inserted in the dolly hitch. Instead, it was still laying on the platform, just where he put it. Apparently, the car was merrily bouncing up and down while the back edges of the ramps were scraping along the highway.

Except for some scratches to the ramps, there was no serious damage. Henry said he now places the pin on the ground beside the connection when unloading his car. I suggested he might want to tie a cord to the pin so that it dangles from the tow bar, a better option than placing it on the ground or hiding it on the platform under the car.

65. DON'T EVEN TRY TO THINK LIKE A MOUSE

Alice lives in the country and parks her Class A alongside her house. One day, she noticed mouse droppings in and around the heater vents as well as in a couple of cabinets. Occasionally, she could actually hear a mouse scurrying through the duct system. She thought, "If the mouse found its way into the duct, it can find its way out with a little persuasion so if I turn on the furnace, the heat will encourage it to come out." She was very wrong! Within 15 minutes, she smelled burnt fur and for several days a horrible stench remained.

To eliminate the smell, she had a major portion of the ducting removed (along with the dead mouse carcass), cleaned, and replaced. Alice said she did learn a valuable ($200) lesson: "Never assume that I know what a mouse might be thinking!"

64. MICE ARE NICE—OUTSIDE

One of our camping neighbors had left his trailer for a few weeks in the fall. Upon his return, mouse droppings were scattered throughout his living areas, and some of his water lines were chewed through. Fortunately, he had turned off his outside tap.

Ron assumed mice had entered through a port where his water hose came into a utility compartment. From there, they likely crawled into the basement and found their way into the salon. After vacuuming up the droppings and repairing the damaged water lines, Ron set traps, catching one little critter, which he released—outside.

Helpful hints: Check for small openings under your rig, especially where the water hose and TV cables enter. Mice can enter through an opening as small as ¼ inch, about the size of a pencil eraser. Pack the openings tightly with steel wool or a portion of an SOS pad. For additional protection, spray with a mixture of peppermint oil and water, a proven mouse-repellant.

63. LOOK BEFORE YOU LEAP

Night had fallen in the campground when Anita decided to leave the coach to bring in their tablecloth from the picnic table. Outside was pitch dark as she did not want to attract moths to their door light. The step switch was set so that the steps would extend when the door opened and retract when the door closed. It always worked that way—until that night.

Anita opened the door and stepped down—and farther down until she landed on the ground. Fortunately, her only injury was a bruised ankle that took the brunt of the fall. The steps had remained retracted.

A nearby RV-repair shop replaced a faulty door switch. Even though the steps now extend reliably when the door is opened, Anita follows the advice in the Instruction Manual: Always look down to make sure the steps are extended before stepping out.

62. LET THERE BE LIGHT

Arriving at a friend's home after dark in his new Class A, Danny asked if he could use a garden hose to fill his freshwater tank. Leaving his flashlight inside the coach, he hurriedly attached the hose and busied himself with other things. About 20 minutes later, he heard the reassuring sound of water coming out of the overflow. When he went to turn off the faucet, he noticed brown waste matter running down both sides of his coach. Inside, he discovered the same stinking mess running out of the bathroom onto the carpets the full length of the motorhome. **OOPS!**

Danny had mistakenly attached the garden hose to his blackwater-flush inlet, which he said was "frighteningly close to the freshwater inlet." Had he used a flashlight, he might have noted the decal: "Do Not Use Flush Unless Black Water Valve is Open."

In the short term, Danny hired professional carpet cleaners. In the long term, he solved the problem by purchasing a larger motorhome with the freshwater intake and blackwater-flush intake in separate compartments. Now he just has to remember which intake is in which compartment!

61. DIESEL PUSHER

Towing your dinghy in gear, with the steering locked, or with the emergency brake on are three expensive mistakes (as we'll see later under Dumber Things) that can easily be avoided by using a checklist, attached to your driver's seat visor. The following somewhat unique mishap suggests a fourth item to add to your checklist.

Bill had filled up his diesel pusher the night before leaving the campground so he could make it all the way home, 400 miles, nonstop. At the crack of dawn, he packed up the coach, attached the tow car, and hit the road.

His family greeted him as he pulled up in front of his house and turned off the engine. But everyone heard an engine still running. **OOPS!** In his haste to leave, Bill hadn't shut off the tow vehicle's engine. Jokingly, his young son asked, "Did the car push the coach all the way home?"

60. SEPARATION OF DUTIES

Eric and his wife, Julie, long-time RVers, were preparing to leave a campground. In the proess, they found a level spot to hook up their Jeep Cherokee. Eric typically did the outside hook up while Julie took care of the inside, ensuring that the gearshift was in Neutral and the emergency brake was off.

Slowly pulling onto the road, the first thing he saw in his outside mirror was his own Jeep! "For some inexplicable reason," Eric had inadvertently connected only one side of the tow bar. In his own words: "It took a half-hour to pound and pry the bent tow bar off of the rig. Had to order a new arm for the Blue Ox and wait two weeks for it. A humbling experience that only cost $180. Now, we double-check each other every time we get underway."

> **Helpful hint:** Double-checking on each other may take a few minutes but will pay dividends. Many of these oopsies would not have occurred if someone had checked to make sure each arrival or departure duty had been completed properly.

59. LIFE IS NOT A BEACH

The Oregon coast has a number of access points for driving onto beautiful sandy beaches. Harry decided to do just that with his truck camper to check out the possibility of camping for free with a view of the ocean. He drove on the beach for about ten minutes when he noticed a little cove that might be a good spot to tuck in for the night. As he approached, he decided to stop and check it out. Unfortunately, when he got back in to move farther into the cove, his rear tires dug into the sand. The more the tires spun, the deeper he sank until he was up to the rear axle. Without a shovel, he used a leveling board to scrape the sand away in front of the rear tires. No luck. He was firmly stuck below the high-water line about two hours away from the ocean filling the inside of his truck.

Without a cellphone, Harry frantically ran to a nearby house to see if he could phone for a tow. The owner had a 4-wheel drive and said he would pull him out. That didn't work so he called a friend who also had a 4-wheel drive. Together, they pulled the truck onto hard sand, stopped, and disconnected the towlines. Harry offered to pay, but they said they were just happy to help. After a big "thank you," Harry drove back to the entrance onto the beach and, without stopping, continued onto the blacktop. After driving to a nearby parking lot to spend the night (free, but without a view of the ocean), Harry said, "I will never again take my truck camper on a sandy beach."

It's just as well: While it may be legal to drive and get stuck on an Oregon beach, overnight camping is prohibited, which is a good thing considering that high tides and sneaky waves could put a damper on your RV experience!

58. BLACK AND BLUE TOAD

While traveling across Canada in their older motorhome, Sid and his wife stopped for fuel and topped up the oil. Four hours later at a rest stop, Sid did a walkaround. **OOPS!** The back of their coach and their once blue Jeep tow vehicle were blanketed with oil. Opening the engine cover, Sid noticed the oil-fill cap was missing. None of the local truck stops or RV dealers he phoned had a proper cap.

Being a handy kind of guy, Sid fashioned a cap by cutting an aluminum can in half and attaching it over the fill hole with a 2-inch gear strap. He then spent hours cleaning off a gallon of oil that had sprayed out of the fill hole. Unfortunately, the next leg of their trip resulted in the same outcome—another gallon of oil covering their toad and back section of the motorhome. Upon inspection, engine vibrations had worn out the aluminum can, which allowed oil to again spray out of the fill hole.

Undeterred, Sid folded a plastic sandwich bag into quarters and attached it with the gear clamp. Even though the bag pulsated with the pressure, it held for the remainder of their 6-week trip, when he was able to get a replacement cap. But the saga continued. On their annual trip south, Sid topped up the oil and a few hours later, another shower of oil. This time, Sid found the cap lying on the inside of the engine compartment. "I'm sure I replaced it after adding oil. On a positive note, after three oil baths, our Jeep will never rust!"

As a preventative measure, Sid drilled a hole in one of the cap handles and attached a plastic zip-tie so the cap would hang near the fill hole as a reminder to replace and tighten it.

Helpful hint: Always replace and securely tighten the oil-fill cap after adding oil ... when you think it's tight, keep tightening!

57. SEEING BLACK SPOTS

Ernie and Marilyn bought a four-year-old motorhome that came with an outside carbon filter that attached to the water intake hose. They often filled their freshwater tank through the filter prior to boondocking. One day, Ernie noticed that their water pressure was quite low and thought that maybe it was time to replace the filter. He did so, but the pressure remained low.

Ernie dismantled the water pump and found the filter screen clogged with black carbon. Apparently, the old filter, which had been used well beyond its replacement date, had ruptured internally, allowing carbon to escape into the water. Cleaning it made some difference but not for long since bits of carbon in their freshwater tank continued to clog the pump screen. After repeatedly filling and emptying their tank, the water pressure was back to normal even though black spots occasionally showed up in their drinking water for weeks afterward.

> **Helpful hint:** Follow the manufacturer's suggestions for replacing your water filter, at least annually if you use your RV regularly, to ensure clean drinking water.

56. BUMPERS ARE FOR BUMPING

While touring Alaska in his motorhome, Roger had missed a turn off and continued on until he found a small gravel parking lot. It looked big enough to turn around so he made a tight U-turn in the lot and powered up a steep incline to get back on the highway. Unfortunately, because of the small lot, he was angled slightly off to one side of the exit. **CRUNCH!**

The bottom right corner of his bumper caught the gravel and broke a weld, causing the bumper to hang low on that side. Had he been able to approach the exit straight on, the bumper would have cleared the gravel. Roger said he continued on his journey for a few more weeks with the front end "looking like it was permanently scowling!"

55. PITCH THE FORK

Pulling into a campground, Don was told to find a vacant site and inform the staff later. Making a sharp right turn into a pull-through site, he watched his Jeep dinghy in the mirror trailing a little to the right. Suddenly, the right front tire "jerked oddly, followed by a scraping sound."

The tire had rolled over a pitchfork hidden in the grass, which skewered the Jeep's right front fender lodging itself in the underbelly of the fender next to the tire! How it got in the grass was a mystery; the office staff had no idea.

Helpful hint: Always inspect your site before pulling onto it just in case there's a pitchfork hiding in the grass! You'll also have a better idea of the location of the facilities (power, water, sewer) and any obstacles.

54. FRAYED BELTS LEAD TO FRAYED NERVES

Mark owned an older Class A with a gasoline engine. At his last oil change, the mechanic suggested some additional work, including replacing the fan belt, which was slightly frayed. Mark decided to "replace it next time," which proved to be a big mistake.

A few months later, Mark was taking his family on a camping trip. While driving to the campground, he heard a loud sound in the engine compartment: **PWANG!** He decided to stop and investigate, but quickly realized his brakes didn't work. Fortunately, he was on a long stretch of highway, which allowed him to slow down and pull off alongside the road. A broken fan belt had destroyed the hydraulic lines and electrical wiring that activated his brakes.

Mark managed to drive slowly several miles to an RV repair shop, using his emergency brake to stop when necessary. There he was able to obtain the necessary repairs to continue on to his destination. "I was just lucky that I didn't have to stop in a hurry," he said.

Yes, he was. In retrospect, Mark agreed that replacing a faulty fan belt was a small price to pay to protect his family, his motorhome, and his sanity.

53. BLACKWATER ON ICE

Grant and his wife had been camping in freezing temperatures in Minnesota before heading south for the winter. Along the way, they pulled into a Truck Stop to drain their blackwater tank. Next to them was a fellow camper who was also dumping. After hooking up his sewer hose, Grant pulled the drain valve. Smelly effluent began spraying out of cracks in his hose, all over the fellow camper. **OOPS!**

They laugh about it now but no one, especially the fellow camper, was laughing then. Profuse apologies followed the incident. Apparently, the plastic hose already had some cracks in it, and an accumulation of ice at the elbow impeded the flow of sewage down the drain. It had to go somewhere! Since then, Grant always checks his hose for cracks before dumping, especially after camping in freezing temperatures.

52. ON THE FLY

Driving to Alaska in a motorhome was high on Doug and Barb's bucket list. On a visit to western Canada, they rented a Class C and within a few days were on the fabled Alaska Highway. On day three, they caught up to a pickup truck carrying an aluminum fishing boat in the back. Rather than pass, Doug slowed down and kept pace with the truck. On a bumpy section of roadway, the boat suddenly became airborne and landed in the middle of the highway. Doug quickly swerved to the left, but hit the boat on its first bounce with the grille and right front bumper. **KABOOM!**

The boat went bouncing off the road, and Doug pulled over to assess the damage to their motorhome. Meanwhile, the driver of the pickup was backing up to retrieve his boat and apologize for the mishap: "Sorry, I guess I should have tied it down."

After exchanging personal information with the driver, Doug and Barb continued their journey with a scratched bumper, smashed-in grille, and broken headlight. In hindsight, Doug admitted, "I was probably following too closely."

Helpful hint: When following a vehicle with an exposed load, either pass, if it is safe to do so, or give yourself some extra stopping space in case the load ends up on the highway.

51. BLACKWATER SHOWER

Jim and his wife had been boondocking in their Class C for a couple of days before arriving at an RV park. Friends had invited them to dinner, so they immediately spruced up upon arrival. Since he had some time before dinner, Jim decided to hook up the sewer hose to drain the black- and gray-water tanks. He got out the hose and inserted one end into the sewer drain. Holding the other end, he rotated the cap from the discharge pipe. **WOOSH!**

Blackwater shot out all over Jim, who didn't even try to attach the hose until the gusher decreased to a dribble. He sheepishly admitted, "I forgot to close the blackwater valve while we were dry camping," adding, "We were late for dinner!"

Helpful hint: In addition to a blackwater valve, it's prudent to have a separate gate-valve at the end of the discharge pipe, which is kept closed when boondocking and in transit.

Larry MacDonald, Ph.D.

DUMBER THINGS

Larry MacDonald, Ph.D.

50. PARTING IS SUCH SORROW

Ed was just about ready to leave his campsite with his fifth-wheel trailer. The campsite was on a one-way lane that he had to block with his truck while attaching the trailer. One car had just gotten there, and the driver asked, "How long are you going to be?" Ed replied, "About five minutes." He continued to back up. When he heard a click, he assumed his kingpin was firmly attached to the hitch. Ed's normal routine at this point was to check the hitch-lock and attach his breakaway-switch cable, which he figured he would do after getting out of the other guy's way. He quickly raised the front jacks, closed the tailgate, and proceeded to pull forward. **KABOOM!**

The latch hadn't closed and locked around the kingpin so the truck moved but the trailer didn't. The kingpin extension landed on the top of the tailgate, causing some serious dents and bending it backward. Ed, who was obviously a really nice guy, apologized to the driver who was waiting and said it would take longer than five minutes! The driver turned around and left. Had Ed initially followed his normal routine of checking the hitch-lock, he would have prevented this mishap.

After a thorough assessment of the situation, Ed lowered the front jacks and reattached the kingpin to the hitch, this time making sure that the hitch was firmly closed and locked. He also attached the breakaway-switch cable and raised the front jacks. The tailgate was damaged so badly it couldn't be opened. Ed's creative solution after returning home was to remove his bent tailgate permanently, which he considered "an inexpensive alternative to the airflow models designed to improve mileage."

49. TOW WOES

Before leaving a campground, Don hooked up his tow car to the motorhome, something he had done many times over the years. After about 100 miles of freeway driving, he pulled into a rest stop and noticed that the left front tire of his tow car was in shreds. The right front tire was also damaged, but not as badly. Assessing the situation, Don realized that he had forgotten to unlock the steering wheel by turning the ignition key to the ACC position.

After installing his spare, he drove home, unaware that he had forgotten to release the emergency brake of his tow car. As a result, both rear brakes burned out. Don lamented, "I was not a happy camper," a phrase often associated with RV Oopsies. The cost of two tires, wheel alignment, and rear brakes came to over $500.

Since this mishap, Don has prudently added "Steering Wheel" and "Parking Brake" to his Departure Checklist. Based on the next incident, he might also have added "Shift Lever in Neutral."

48. A REALLY HOT DAY IN DEATH VALLEY

Larry (not the author!) and Linda were headed toward Death Valley National Park towing a VW Baja Bug behind their motorhome. Their route included a very curvy road that precluded towing, so they disconnected. Larry drove the motorhome; Linda followed in the car. At the end of the curvy section, they hooked up. Linda said, "It's in Neutral, and the brake is off."

In the interest of marital harmony, Larry chose not to check. Off they went at 50 mph. Nearing the top of a hill, Larry throttled back and felt an immediate resistance. Looking in the mirror, he saw flames and smoke billowing from the tow car. After pulling over and extinguishing the flames, he discovered that the car was in gear. The mechanical fuel pump, combined with the overheated engine, started a fire that consumed the entire rear end of the car. They continued their somewhat subdued excursion into Death Valley with the gearshift of their non-functional tow car in Neutral.

Larry and Linda have since bought another tow car, and in the interest of marriage harmony they have agreed to check on each other as to whether it's in Neutral with the brake off.

RV OOPSIES

47. JACKS ARE HIGH

Dean arrived at his campsite with his fifth-wheel and decided to unhook the truck. He blocked the trailer tires, unlocked the hitch, disconnected the electrical and brake cables, opened the tailgate, and pulled forward. **KA-BOOM!** The front of the trailer came crashing down, making V-shaped dents in the side rails of the truck bed and some noticeable symmetrical grooves in the underside of the trailer. **OOPS!** He had forgotten to lower the front jacks.

After a few choice words, Dean extended the front jacks. His long-term solution was to have the bent side rails repaired. Rather than fix the grooves, Dean used them as irritating reminders to always lower the front jacks before pulling away the truck.

46. SO-LOW

Helen drives a Class C and often goes RVing on her own. At a campground where she had a reservation, she decided to just back into the assigned site without first checking it out. Looking in both side mirrors, she slowly backed up. When just about ready to stop, she heard **CRUNCH!**

The top rear of her rig bumped into a very large tree branch, breaking three top lights and scraping the roof. A Ranger got there right after. "If I only had gotten here two minutes earlier, I could have warned you," he said.

He then helped her get situated properly, only to find out it was a *pull-in* site. In Helen's own words, "How dumb is that?"

I'm thinking, "Dumber than Dumb!"

> **Helpful hints:** Always check out a site before pulling in to ensure there are no obstacles (trees, tree limbs, posts, picnic tables, fire rings, pitchforks), to assess location of the facilities (power, water, sewer), and to determine clearance for slide-outs. If you're driving solo, wait two minutes for a Ranger or ask a fellow camper to serve as a spotter.

45. A FALLING APPLE

Sharon's husband, who refused to give his name, left his new laptop computer on the dining table; then headed down the highway in their Class A. An unexpected panic stop resulted in all unsecured items, including the computer, becoming airborne projectiles. **WHAM!** His Apple computer was damaged beyond repair, a $3,000 lesson in Newton's first law of motion, paraphrased: "An object in motion, at 60 mph, tends to remain in motion until it smacks into a wall during a panic stop."

Sharon and her anonymous husband now make sure that all loose objects are secure before they get underway. I reassured Sharon they are not alone. I've yet to meet a single RVer who hasn't broken a wine glass, candleholder, coffee cup, or something else that should have been safely tucked away prior to getting underway. Such minor mishaps don't qualify for an Oops Award, but a smashed computer? That qualifies!

44. PATIENCE IS A VIRTUE

Having just returned home from a solo weekend camping trip in his new Class A, Charles decided to back into his gated RV pad alongside his house. He blocked open the steel gate; then got back inside and proceeded to back up. Within a few seconds ... **RIPPPP!** A quick assessment showed that the gate had partially closed by the wind; grabbing the rear compartment door and peeling the coach open like a tin can. Several months and $8,000 later, his rig was like new again.

Now, here's the sad part. Had Charles waited 30 minutes, his son would have been home to assist as a spotter, preventing this mishap from ever occurring.

43. A SPOTTER IS ALSO A VIRTUE

Jacob lives on a seldom-traveled rural road and was planning to back his coach into his driveway between two stone pillars. Imbedded in the pillars were upturned angle irons, intended to support a gate, which had yet to be installed. While Jacob was slowly maneuvering his rig backward, it stopped before he cleared the road and seemed to be hung up on something. Wouldn't you know it? A rare traffic jam was forming on the road—two cars from one direction and one from the other.

Frustrated and annoyed, Jacob "poured the coal to her" to pull across the road so that traffic could pass. **KABOOM!** What he was hung up on was one of the angle irons, which had become wedged in the passenger-side rear panel. As he zoomed ahead, the rear panel ripped off, and the pillar was dragged down. The bill for RV repairs came to $8,500 plus the cost of rebuilding the pillar.

Helpful hint: ALWAYS have someone watching behind your rig when backing up, ideally with communication headsets, to provide direction. Of all the hints provided in this book, this one should be engraved in your memory bank.

42. RVING ON THE EDGE

Ron and his wife, Linda, got a late start in their Class A, and darkness fell before they reached their next campground. Misinterpreting directional signs, they found themselves driving into the mountains on a narrow two-lane road in the pitch dark. Coming to a large pullout on the opposite side of the road, Ron attempted to make a U-turn. When the front end of the coach was at the edge of a drop-off, the tow car was still across the road. In a moment of confusion, both Linda and he got up to unhitch the car so they could back up the RV. Opening the door, she noticed the ground moving slowly beneath the steps and yelled, "We're moving!"

Ron ran back up front and put on the emergency brake, but it was too late. The front wheels of the RV went over the edge, causing the front end of the tow car to rise four feet in the air. Fortunately, the brakes of the coach prevented them from going completely over the embankment.

Shortly thereafter, a woman came along who called the police and explained the predicament. A tow company arrived with two trucks. After disconnecting the tow car, they grabbed the RV from behind and pulled it back on level ground while a sheriff-controlled traffic.

What happened here? In his panic, Ron said, "I simply forgot to apply the emergency brake or put the gearshift in Park. I may have moved it to Neutral, but I'm not sure."

The bill included a $500 deductible to cover towing charges as well as the cost of replacing a broken step and tow bar. It could have been much worse.

This lucky couple now has some new rules:

- stop traveling before dark;
- ask for directions when in doubt; and
- learn their turning radius with and without the tow car.

41. YOU HAVE MAIL

Russ had bought a new motorhome and was attempting to back it out of his driveway without a spotter. Just as his back tires neared the opposite curb, he felt the rig lurch and heard a loud **CRUNCH!** Thinking he had just bumped into the mailbox across the street, Russ angrily and hastily pulled forward. Not a good move! Yes, the mailbox had been knocked off, but worse, the 4" x 4" post embedded in concrete was pushed down well under the rear quarter. The forward movement resulted in an even louder **CRUNCH** when the post, acting like a spear, pierced the flooring and tore out portions of the rear bedroom, exhaust system, and rear wall. The repair bill came to over $5,000.

> **Helpful hint:** If you happen to back into something, immediately stop and assess the situation. Often, more severe damage occurs in the process of pulling forward. Better yet, avoid backing into something by using a spotter. Are you starting to see a theme here?

40. HOLA SHOULDER

After a relaxing winter on the sunny beaches of Baja, Mexico, William joined a caravan of motorhomes heading for the U.S. border. The northbound lane was quite narrow—9½ feet of pavement—with a 6-inch drop off onto a "shoulder" littered with rocks and other debris. Along the way, an impatient motorist attempted to pass and was forced to cut in sharply to avoid an oncoming truck. To prevent being sideswiped, William drove off the road and onto the rocks, eventually stopping after a very scary and bumpy ride. Fortunately, no one was injured, and he was able to continue with the caravan for the remainder of the trip. At home, after repairing a bent frame and numerous dents and scratches, an RV dealer handed William a bill for $10,000.

In this instance, William did most of the right things, including traveling in a caravan when in Mexico. Had he not moved over or lost control on the rocky shoulder, the outcome might have been disastrous. For that, he is to be congratulated!

On the other hand, this mishap could have been avoided. William was driving his large Class A on a narrow road with a severe drop-off and inadequate shoulder. Talk about RVing on the edge!

> **Helpful hint:** In our search for adventure, we must always be aware of road conditions—too narrow, soft, wet, slippery, or steep—that may be unsafe for large, heavy RVs. Avoidance is always the best option.

39. SWING YOUR PARTNER, NOT YOUR TAIL

Art and his wife were driving south for the winter in their Class A motorhome when they decided to overnight in the parking lot of a big-box store. Art circled the lot and was driving parallel to a retaining wall on the passenger side when he noticed a suitable parking space to his left. As he turned sharply, a loud **RIPPP** came from behind.

Looking over his shoulder, Art could see directly out the back of his coach. The right rear corner had gotten caught on a protruding angle iron, opening up the back end like a can of sardines. After a sleepless night, he drove slowly to a nearby RV dealer who pushed the back wall into position and secured it with brackets and screws. Continuing on to their destination, Art had it fixed properly by another RV dealer to the tune of $20,000.

Tail-swing can be problematic for RVers with large rigs. To emphasize this point, I've included the following mishap that also resulted from tail swing.

38. POST TRAUMATIC SYNDROME

I was recently in a campground where each site is numbered on a 3-foot-tall 8" x 8" wooden post, anchored in concrete at the entrance to the site. While camped in a corner site, I watched a brand-new Class A arrive, which was headed for the pull-through site directly across the road from us. When I say "brand new," I mean that the owners had just picked it up at an RV dealership a few miles away, and this was their first outing.

The front left side of the coach was already past our post when the driver stopped to let his wife out so she could make sure they cleared a tree on the right side. It was obvious to her that some branches would scrape their new rig unless he turned sharply left so she motioned for him to turn, a bit more, just a bit more … "OK, you're good to go!"

Having cleared the tree, the driver then was in a position to turn right and enter the site. **CRUNCH!**

"What the hell was that?" he hollered to his wife.

They both came around to the driver's side and saw our post pushed over and a major tear in the rear left side of their coach. I hadn't seen the actual contact with the post, but I did see a grown man cry after he realized what had happened. He hadn't accounted for tail swing to the left as he turned sharply right to enter the site.

The gentleman called the dealership about the damage, and they suggested he bring it back in for repairs, which pretty much ended what might have been a lovely maiden voyage. Based on feedback I've received from other RVers, tail swing results in many posts and stop signs being hit while in the process of turning, often in campgrounds, parking lots, and gas stations where space is tight.

> **Helpful hint:** For each three feet of overhang beyond the rear wheels, expect one foot of tail swing. Thus, 15 feet of overhang can result in five feet of tail swing. It's instructive to line up the left side of your coach or trailer with a white line in a parking lot, turn sharply to the right, and move very slowly forward while someone watches and tells you to stop when the rear of your rig reaches the maximum distance from the line. Awareness of how much your tail swings will make it less likely you'll hit those posts and stop signs.

37. IT'S THE REAL THING

Mathew had owned a Class A for years without problems. This year, however, he began hearing a clunking sound that only occurred occasionally when accelerating or braking. He took it to an RV dealer who suggested it might be the brakes, driveshaft, or maybe the transmission. They did some work on the brakes, which didn't fix the problem, so he took it to another shop and then another.

After several thousand dollars of repair bills, Mathew figured it was time to sell before whatever it was got worse. While sprucing up his motorhome by vacuuming under the front seat, he found a full can of Coke that had been clunking back and forth against the seat frame. Problem solved. Mathew sheepishly admitted, "After all those repairs, I decided not to sell."

36. THE WHEEL GOES 'ROUND … HOPEFULLY

Tony was driving in their older-model Class C motorhome when his wife said, "I think I smell something."

Within minutes after slowing down, a loud **CLUNK** and **SCRAPE** came from the rear of their coach, which jarred to a stop as if someone had thrown out an anchor. The passenger-side rear wheel had come off the axle, wich was now sitting on the ground.

A Truck Service Center later diagnosed the problem: The wheel bearings seized to the axle after overheating, likely a result of inadequate lubrication. The total bill, including a rebuilt axle, came to $5,000. Tony said, "Fortunately the differential wasn't damaged since it's nearly impossible to get major parts for a 25-year-old motorhome."

Even more fortunately, the wheel didn't fall off at high speed, which may have damaged a lot more than the differential.

> **Helpful hint:** Since regular maintenance is nearly always less costly than occasional repairs, consider servicing your RV at intervals recommended in your Owner's Manual.

35. PUMPS AND BUMPS

This past summer, Neil learned a very important lesson about using fuel stations. He pulled his 35-foot motorhome alongside the inside pumps and filled up. He then began his exit by turning to the right. Hearing a "funny sound," he immediately stopped and got out to investigate. Lo and behold, a car had pulled up along his passenger side for gas.

According to Neil, "It was not a pretty sight." The car was scraped from the driver's door to the front bumper ($1,400) and his side compartments were badly scraped and dented ($4,000). To quote Neil, he will "never, never, never again get gas at an inside pump and will wait as long as it takes to access an outside pump, which provides more room to maneuver." That's sound advice for all drivers of large rigs who access fuel stations on a regular basis.

34. WHAT'S ON TV

Not long ago, I was casually watching a couple packing up their motorhome, preparing to leave their pull-through site. Everything was going according to plan: hoses and cables were disconnected and stored. And then they got in and drove away. Left behind was their disconnected satellite dish, standing on a tripod about 20 feet away from the pad. The next morning, I informed the Campground Office, and the dish was subsequently removed, hopefully later claimed by its owner.

Confession time: Nearly every RVer has left something behind when leaving a campsite—usually small items like a doormat, tablecloth, faucet fitting, or leveling blocks. In almost every case, they simply didn't inspect the site *after* pulling out. But forgetting something as important as a satellite dish qualifies this anonymous couple for a Dumber Award.

33. IN THE HOT SEAT

Rod and Lynn's motorhome had a table lamp plugged into a timer. Arriving at a campground, Rod temporarily placed the lamp with the shade removed onto the driver's seat while he hooked up the power cable, water hose, and sewer line. In the process of opening their slides, Lynn yelled frantically, "Our coach is filling with smoke!"

Apparently, the timer decided it was time for the light to come on while the lamp was laying on the seat. **OOPS!**

The heated bulb melted the leatherette and burned a large hole in the seat, which Rod and Lynn covered with a blanket until a new seat could be installed at a cost of $600. Rod confessed, "I was in the hot seat for some time after that one."

32. I GO WHERE I'M TOWED TO … USUALLY

Driving his motorhome on a side road, David noted a sign "Uneven Railroad Crossing" and slowed to 35 mph—still too fast. A severe jounce prompted a quick check of the rear-view monitor. The tow car appeared to be following along normally so David proceeded to a campground. Upon inspection, David found that every hanger in the rear closet had jumped off the rod. Even worse, the trailer hitch was bent downward. The next day, being close to home, David decided to drive "as tenderly as possible."

On the final stretch of freeway, David was driving under the posted speed limit in the right lane when he and his wife, Daryl, heard a disturbing **CLUNK-A-CLUNK**. Daryl looked at the rear-view monitor and yelled, "The Jeep isn't attached!"

David immediately pulled over onto the right-hand shoulder and prepared to stop. They watched in horror as their Jeep passed them and headed across two lanes of heavy traffic, onto a narrow strip of median, and continued along the guardrail for about a quarter-mile before stopping. When the hitch fell off, the triangular tow-bar assembly dropped to the ground and folded back under, acting as a rudder to keep the vehicle headed mostly straight ahead. The split-ring fastener on the breakaway switch had also failed so the brakes were not applied. Safety chains, attached to the hitch, went along for the ride.

Shortly afterward, the police arrived and stopped traffic while David drove the wayward Jeep over to the right-hand shoulder where he detached the tow bar. Considering the damages and injuries that might have resulted from their Jeep's first solo flight, this couple was lucky: A new hitch, tow bar assembly, and some structural and cosmetic body work came to only $2,500. Isn't it amazing that a trailer hitch rated at 10,000 pounds can fail after just one jounce?

> **Helpful hint:** Driving, no matter how tenderly, with a bent hitch or tow bar is not recommended, especially on a freeway!

31. BLUB, BLUB, BLUB

Jeff and Gaylene enjoy camping in their Class A diesel pusher. Since they also enjoy fishing, they would often tow a small boat on a trailer. One day, they decided to launch the boat near a lakeside campground. Jeff undid the straps holding the boat to the trailer and remained in the boat while Gaylene backed the coach down the launch ramp. When the boat was just floating off the trailer, Jeff yelled "**STOP!**" but the coach kept moving backward—so far that water covered the engine causing it to stall. Neither of them got wet, but their coach sure did — nearly up to the driver's seat.

What happened isn't exactly clear. Gaylene maintains that when she put the brakes on, the coach kept moving backward. Did she inadvertently push on the accelerator instead of the brake pedal? Did the brakes stop working? Or were the brakes ineffective because the ramp was slippery? What we do know is that they called for a very large tow truck to haul their coach and trailer out of the water. They also paid a very large bill to get their rig ready for their next camping trip. Jeff insisted, "Never again will we launch our boat with the motorhome; we'll fish from shore if we have to."

30. NASCAR IN THE REAR VIEW

Pulling a boat trailer with his Class C, Norm hit a dip in the highway and immediately heard a loud **BANG**. He looked in his rear-view mirror and saw what "looked like a NASCAR race complete with smoke and swerving cars." Pulling over to the side, he got out to see what had happened.

It all started back home when Norm purchased a 16-inch hitch extender to accommodate his family's four bikes on a rack between the RV and the boat. When he hit the dip, the weight of the bikes put downward pressure on the extended hitch, snapping two of the four bolts and forcing it down toward the road. The brunt of the impact was taken by the trailer's spare tire mounted near the hitch. The tire tore and smoked, causing havoc on the highway as cars swerved to avoid the shredded rubber. Fortunately, no one was injured.

A wrecker towed the boat to their campground, where Norm removed the extender and installed a new hitch and tire at a cost of $500. Norm has since learned that an extender can reduce hitch capacity by up to 50%; adding the weight of four bikes reduces it even more. He now carries two of his bikes in the boat and hangs two on a rack attached to the RV ladder.

> **Helpful hints:** Carrying two full-size bikes on an aluminum RV ladder might result in a bent ladder (it did for me). As an alternative when towing a trailer, consider installing a front-mounted bike rack.

29. Y BACK UP

When Yogi and Judy purchased their new Class A motorhome, the dealer advised them to never back up without a spotter at the back at the coach.

Of course, RVers already know that, don't we? A year into their RVing adventures, they pulled into a small campground with a narrow, slightly uphill entrance leading to the office. After checking in, they disconnected the tow vehicle. and Judy drove it to their assigned site back down the hill. They agreed that Yogi would wait for her return.

After parking the car, Judy started walking back up the hill. Tired of waiting, Yogi decided to back down on his own. Using his side mirrors, he could see clearly both sides of the road. What he didn't realize is that the road branched in the shape of a Y and what he was looking at was the left and right sides of two different roads. At the junction of the Y was a large tree, which stopped the coach abruptly before Judy could warn him. As she got to the driver's side window, Yogi shrieked, "I don't get it; I could see the whole road so I'm not sure what I hit."

She calmly replied, "You hit a tree, which wasn't on the road!"

More than $1,300 later, with the dealer's advice now engrained in their brains, the coach was like new again.

Helpful hint: Always, always, always use a spotter when backing up … what you can't see can stop you abruptly (Is that starting to sound like a familiar theme?).

28. MMM, MMM, NOT SO GOOD

With the recent increase in fuel prices, Floyd was concerned about fuel costs for their diesel pusher. Knowing that a frugal friend had various diesel engines running on biodiesel for half the price of ordinary diesel, Floyd arranged to purchase a 55-gallon drum of it from him. He then pumped the entire contents into their coach's tank, "getting hungry in the process since the fuel smelled like chicken soup."

Due to personal circumstances, Floyd couldn't travel during that summer. However, in November he "cranked her up and took off for parts unknown!"

Parts unknown turned out to be a mile down the road! After a $1,500 tow, the repair facility power-washed and steam-cleaned the fuel tanks, then cleaned the fuel lines and injectors, all for $2,600.

Turns out that the biodiesel was indeed a byproduct of Campbell Soup, which gelled to chicken fat as the weather cooled! Floyd admitted, "I haven't been able to eat chicken soup since that fateful day."

Helpful hint: Although some motorhome engines are designed to run on biodiesel, check with your manufacturer to determine its recommended fuel.

27. BLACKWATER WOES

For whatever reason, some RVers go above and beyond what is needed to clean the inside of their blackwater tank. Here's a story about Henry, a fellow who said he never did anything dumb while RVing—until his wife reminded him otherwise!

After emptying his blackwater tank and running his sewer tank flush for ten minutes in his Class A, Henry wanted to get the blackwater tank "really, really clean." He shut off the discharge valve and ran the flusher for an additional ten minutes, figuring he would fill the tank with water, then drain it along with every speck of crud that was in there. This reasoning occurred in spite of a sign by the flusher inlet: **Caution. Sewer valves must be *open* when using this inlet.** Henry also figured that ten minutes would be enough time to grab a cup of java and sit outside with his wife for a little chat. Immediately upon hearing a loud **BANG**, Henry knew that his ten minutes was up!

Pressure inside the tank broke their toilet valve, and, before Henry could get the flusher water turned off, smelly black water overflowed throughout their coach. After a couple of professional cleanings failed to eliminate the stench, they had all of their carpets replaced. I'm still not sure why Henry couldn't remember doing anything dumb when the bill came to $2,200!

Helpful hints: Never, never, never run the sewer-tank flusher without opening the sewer valves. And don't be obsessed with cleaning the blackwater tank as if you were going to eat lunch down there. Have lunch in the salon instead!

26. HIGHWAY TO HELL

This RV trip starts in the cool, refreshing mountains of Western Canada and ends in the hot, dry city of Las Vegas a few weeks later. John and his wife, Sue, had done some camping in their Class A, mainly in Canada. Sue suggested, and John agreed, that it would be nice to take his mother-in-law to Vegas, a place she had always wanted to visit. Both the roof and the cab air conditioners hadn't worked for some time in their aging motorhome, but that shouldn't be a problem. After all, "How hot can it be in Vegas in August?" These Canadians were about to find out!

All went well as they crossed the border and spent a couple of weeks in the northern mountainous states. The last leg of their trip had them leaving Utah and heading for Vegas. The closer they got, the higher the temperature rose: 90° … 100° … 110° F. The previously cool air blowing through the vents was beginning to feel like the blast from a hair dryer on "Hot." John reported his mother-in-law saying, "Now I know what it would feel like if I drove to Hell." Sue protested loudly: "Why didn't we get the air conditioners fixed in Canada?"

"No worries," John said, "We'll get some ice cubes at the next gas station and place them in front of the vents. That will cool things down."

It did. The temperature dropped from 110° to 100° F, which now felt like a hair dryer on "Medium." When they finally got to Vegas, John was given an ultimatum: Get the air conditioners fixed, or the ladies were flying home to Canada with or without him.

While the ladies played the slots in an air-conditioned casino, John visited several RV-repair shops, dismayed to find out that it was going to cost over $1,200 to totally replace the ceiling unit and install a new compressor in the cab unit. Since the two flights home would likely cost close to that amount, he figured he might as well get them fixed.

They had only budgeted for three days in Vegas. Unfortunately, it required a week to fix the air conditioners. John said he refused to add up the total costs of the repairs, hotel rooms, meals, and gambling losses. As he put it, "I didn't want to know. We had been to Hell and survived. Not many RVers can say that!"

25. WHERE'S THE REMOTE

Carol and her husband had camped in their motorhome for many years. Early on, they had purchased an outdoor-temperature gauge for the inside of their coach. The instructions indicated that the wireless remote temperature sensor be placed in a shady spot and not exposed to moisture. Carol found what she considered the perfect location: on top of the rear wheel. It worked fine as long as she remembered to remove the remote before getting underway, which she did numerous times, except for three occasions. On two of them, as her husband pulled out of the campsite, the remote fell on the ground out of harm's way; they picked it up during their site inspection. On the third, it fell directly in line with the rear tire and was "totally squashed."

Their new remote came with a clip, allowing it to be attached under the front bumper and removed before getting underway. The one-time Carol forgot, the remote fell off "someplace between San Francisco and Sacramento!" She purchased another and now ties a yellow ribbon on the steering wheel to remind her to remove it before moving the motorhome.

> **Helpful hint:** As an alternative means of remembering, consider adding, "Remove Temperature Remote" to a Departure Checklist. However, if you like yellow ribbons, you could still tie one on the steering wheel to remind you to use the Checklist!

24. BEACH-HEAD BOULEVARD

Red Beach in California is a huge sandy beach on the Pacific Ocean used primarily for Camp Pendleton's Marine Corps amphibious exercises. When exercises are underway, tanks and other heavy vehicles use the dirt road to access the beach. As a result, the road is often deeply rutted and difficult to drive on, especially with an RV. Occasionally, back in the day when there were no exercises ongoing, the military base would allow RVers to dry camp on the beach.

One weekend, learning that Red Beach was open, Dave and Caroline packed up their old Class A with all its blemishes and headed down the dirt road. After a particularly jolting spot, Dave happened to look in his right-side mirror, and lo and behold, he saw their tow vehicle peeking back at him. He was towing a VW, which required only a simple tow bar with a coupler attached to the hitch ball on the rear of the RV. Apparently, the coupler had broken loose from the hitch ball, but the safety chains were still towing the car. Dave's immediate reaction was to hit the brakes. **CRUNCH!**

The RV stopped quickly and so did the VW—right into the rear bumper, smashing the left headlight and denting the fender. Today, Dave still RVs with a tow vehicle, but it is properly equipped with a baseplate, tow bar, and a supplemental braking and breakaway system.

23. WELCOME TO PLEASANT VIEW

Not long after purchasing his new Class A, Bruce arranged to meet some friends for a weekend of camping. He decided to go to the campground a day early to settle in and make preparations for his friends' arrival. Driving along a narrow two-lane road far out in the country, he noticed the sign for the campground just as he passed the entrance. Not being able to back up with his motorcycle trailer attached, he continued on, looking for a place to turn around. Finally, he came to a church with a graveyard, which had a paved driveway around it. "Perfect," he thought!

Scoping out the driveway, he noticed a small hump at the entrance, which might cause his trailer hitch to drag, but he "figured it was worth a little dragging not to have to drive farther down the road." As he entered the cemetery, Bruce was anticipating the sound of the hitch hitting the pavement. Instead, he heard a loud **RIPPP** sound from overhead. He immediately stopped and looked over his right shoulder, amazed to see a hole in the ceiling where his air conditioner used to be. While focusing his attention on the hump, he failed to notice the 12-foot overhead iron arch "Pleasant View Gardens," previously supported by two brick pillars. The arch was lying on top and the brick pillars were leaning against the sides of his coach.

A couple of hours later, after cleaning up the mess and leaving his personal information at the church, he drove to the campground with the wind whistling through the hole where his air conditioner used to be. Bruce said he saved some of the iron letters from the arch to serve as a reminder of his misadventure.

When his friends arrived the next day, he described the mishap and showed them the damage, which resulted in some chuckles and one lame comment: "Well, at least you made it out of the cemetery!"

22. BLOWN WITH THE WIND

Jack and his wife were offered the use of his brother's Class C motorhome for a camping trip in the Palm Springs area. Since they were novice RVers, Jack's brother carefully went through all the systems, including how to manually extend and retract the awning. Off they went for a week of camping, with Jack driving the motorhome and his wife following in their car.

Arriving at their campsite on a sunny day, Jack decided to extend the awning to provide shade while they had dinner. Near the end of the week, with the awning still extended, they headed out in their car on a sightseeing trip. While gone, the wind picked up ... really picked up! When they returned, much to their horror, their awning with bent braces was upside down on the roof. Jack got some fellow campers to help him get it back down and secured to the side.

To make things right with his brother, he arranged with a local RV dealer to install a completely new awning at a cost of $800, which his brother agreed to share because he neglected to tell Jack to secure or retract the awning when leaving the campground.

> **Helpful hint:** Awnings are very susceptible to wind damage. If they are not well secured with ground straps, always retract them when leaving the campground for more than a few hours, especially in potentially high-wind locals.

21. THINGS THAT GO BUMP IN THE NIGHT

Greg's relatively new Class A had a large awning, which automatically retracted when it got windy. An anemometer (wind speed indicator), mounted on a pole attached to the roof, sent a signal to the awning motor if the wind speed exceeded a preset value. Greg said he enjoyed this feature if the wind picked up when he wasn't around but not so much when he was barbequing under the awning on a rainy day!

On one of their frequent trips to a State Park for a weekend of relaxation, he and his wife arrived just after dark and chose a site that looked suitable for their coach. With his wife as a spotter at the rear, he backed into the site. Just as he cleared the road, they both heard a **CLUNK** coming from the roof. Looking up, they noticed a low tree branch touching the roof, which they assumed had collided with the air conditioner. No worries, Greg said, he would check it in the morning.

Later that night, it started raining heavily. When they woke up, water was dripping from several ceiling lights in the salon and bedroom. To protect the carpets, they put pans under the drips and emptied them regularly—hardly the relaxing weekend they had anticipated. When the rain finally stopped in late afternoon, Greg climbed up on the roof and saw that the low branch had knocked down his anemometer pole leaving a depression and a hole in the roof. Rain had collected in the depression and ran through the hole onto the ceiling of their coach.

After covering the hole with duct tape, they packed up and returned home. Their RV dealer reattached the anemometer and replaced the entire ceiling, which was costly but covered by insurance since the loss was "sudden and accidental."

> **Helpful hints:** A spotter should look <u>up</u> as well as on the sides and back of the rig to ensure adequate clearance when backing into a campsite. Low branches are especially problematic in smaller and more primitive campgrounds such as state parks.

20. SUCH A DEAL

An elderly gentleman had been living for many years in his older Class A at a Florida RV resort. Unfortunately, because of ill health he had to be admitted to a long-term care facility. He asked his neighbor, Ivor, a snowbird who rented a park model annually, "If you want my coach, you can have it for a dollar, provided you remove it from the site within a week." Although the engine wouldn't start, "it seemed like such a deal" that Ivor couldn't pass it up. For $500, he had it towed to a storage lot, where it remained until the following season for $100 a month.

When Ivor returned south in the fall, he had the motorhome towed to an RV-repair shop. Much to his dismay, it needed major repairs: engine, transmission, brakes, exhaust system, tires, batteries, and the list went on, adding over $30K to the $1 motorhome. Having rebuilt his motorhome to a road-worthy condition, Ivor's limited finances prevented him from "hitting the road." In the end, he was forced to sell it—at a considerable loss.

> **Helpful hint:** If you're thinking of buying an RV at a price that's too good to be true, it probably is! Always have a rig inspected by a qualified mechanic before purchasing.

19. A HURTFUL HOOKUP

This award is rightfully shared between two people: the RVer who reported the mishap and the unwitting "Helper" who caused it.

Getting ready to depart a campground in his coach, Paul was hooking up his tow car when his camping neighbor Ed offered his assistance. As Paul was putting in the left tow-bar pin and hooking up the cables, Ed put in the right pin. About 100 miles down the road, all appeared fine until he crossed a very rough narrow bridge. Immediately afterward, he glanced in the right-side mirror and noticed that his car was riding on the shoulder, as if attempting to pass. Carefully stopping, he went back to discover that the right pin was gone, most likely because Ed had not pushed it all the way in until it locked.

Paul said: "Thinking back on the bridge crossing, if my car had been off to the side just before the bridge, it probably would have climbed the guardrail and landed in the river, not to mention other possible damages to my motorhome."

A scary thought indeed! Fortunately, he was able to obtain a hitch pin nearby and was soon back on the road with his car safely attached behind.

Helpful hint: Don't accept help with departure duties from anyone without checking on their work.

18. CURBS, POSTS, AND MARTINIS

After purchasing some groceries and gin for his favorite drink, David maneuvered his fifth-wheel through the parking lot and cut a corner with a raised concrete curb. His right rear wheels went over the curb and into a recession, followed by a **CRUNCH**! The rear stabilizer jack, just behind the wheels, had caught on the outside of the curb and was bent backward at a severe angle. The story gets better—or worse, depending on your perspective!

After disengaging the jack from the curb, David proceeded to a campground where I (the author) was camped in an adjacent site. While backing into his site, he hit a 12" x 12" wooden post, used to protect the electrical box. While showing me a broken sidelight, scraped paint, and a crack in the fiberglass, his wife insisted, "I hollered for him to stop, but he didn't hear me."

David took me aside and quietly remarked, "I swear she never said a word, but two screw ups in one day definitely justify two martinis, don't you think?"

Actually, since he didn't invite me to join him, I was thinking two screw-ups in one day definitely justify a Dumber Award!

> **Helpful hints:** (1) Use extra caution when driving through parking lots as they are typically designed for cars rather than large RVs. (2) Use a walkie-talkie system (with the volume turned up!) when backing up, and listen to what your spotter is saying.

17. JUST DON'T BACK UP

Doug had packed up his motorhome to leave the campground. After pulling out of his site, he moved over to the side of the road to hook up his Cadillac tow car. After doing so, he realized that he didn't have enough room to make the sharp turn in front of him, so he decided to back up. When he had gone about ten feet, he saw in his rear-view camera that the front wheels of his car were turned almost sideways. However, they straightened out as he pulled forward to leave the campground.

After arriving home and disconnecting his car, he noticed a warning light, "Service All Wheel Drive," on his dashboard, which came on each time he drove the car. His local dealership found that the steering wheel position sensor needed to be replaced, likely a result of the front tires being turned an excessive amount when he backed up in the campground. The cost of a new sensor (over $600) impressed on Doug an important lesson: "Never back up the motorhome when the tow car is attached, even for a short distance." Although he did add, "If my wife had held the steering wheel while I was backing up, none of this would have happened!"

16. HIJACKING

Ian and Judy were the proud owners of a new 33-foot Class A. After driving home from the dealership, Ian parked it very carefully on their short driveway as close as possible to the garage. After examining some of its features, they decided to test the Auto-Level function. Ian was outside to watch but got distracted by an inquisitive neighbor as the coach began leveling. The back end went up … and up … and still more up, tipping the front end closer to the garage. **SMASH**!

The front windshield had collided with a nail protruding from the roof overhang, punching a hole and fracturing an area over a foot in diameter in the glass. Ian said, "We were devastated, so much so that the damage was difficult to see through our tears!"

Two weeks and $2,800 later, they were able to use their coach on their first camping trip, where the leveling system worked just fine.

> **Helpful hint:** As we've seen in previous RV Oopsies, a friendly well-meaning neighbor can distract us at exactly the wrong time. "Can we talk later? I need to pay attention here," would be an appropriate comment to make when you should be focusing on the task at hand.

15. THERE'S A MUDDY ROAD AHEAD

Nate and his family were traveling cross-country in their Class A with a Jeep Cherokee in tow. In North Dakota, because of road construction, they were stopped by a flag person and advised to take a detour to avoid about 25 miles of rough gravel road ahead. To do so meant an additional 50 miles to reach their destination. The flag person was allowing travel on the road but indicated that "neither the state nor the company would be responsible for damages." After a quick calculation of the additional fuel and time required for the detour, Nate decided to go for it. "How bad could it get if other cars and trucks are heading down the road?"

After a few miles, the road got muddy and construction crews were spreading gravel in the slippery spots. It was definitely a white-knuckle drive, with several delays to allow for one-way traffic. Two hours later, they were back on paved highway. Shortly thereafter, they pulled into a Rest Stop to check out the rig. The motorhome was a bit muddy but the Jeep looked like it had gone through a war zone. The entire front end was pockmarked from stones thrown up by the rear tires of the coach. The repair bill, including a new windshield, grille, and headlights, came to over $5,000. Here is Nate's hindsight assessment: "Taking the detour would have saved me both time and money."

Helpful hint: Yogi Berra's quote, "When you come to a fork in the road, take it," can be paraphrased for RVers: "When you come to a detour in the road, take it."

14. THE CHAIN GANG

When it was time to leave a campground, the engine in Archie's motorhome wouldn't start. He called his friend Matt, who had a sizable truck with a ball hitch. Matt graciously agreed to tow it to an RV-repair shop in the nearby town if Archie would purchase a 16-foot chain with hooks, which he did.

They hooked the chain into two holes on the frame of the motorhome and secured it about eight feet away to the ball hitch of the truck. Ever so gently, Matt pulled the coach out of the campground, with Archie at the wheel. Down the road they went until they got to a crossroad with a stop sign. The truck stopped but the motorhome kept on rolling, until it banged hard against the truck's hitch, smashing the lower front panel of the motorhome. Archie said, "The brakes didn't work."

Rather than risk more damage, they called for a tow truck—to the tune of $400.

Helpful hint: Never tow a motorhome (or any vehicle for that matter) on your own, especially with a chain. Tow trucks are better equipped and operators assume liability for towing damage.

13. A HUMAN WHEEL-CHOCK

Ray and his friend Ralph had both arrived at the same campground in separate RVs. Ray had already set up when Ralph came over to tell him that his engine would not turn over and start after he had parked to have a look at his site. After checking the battery and fuses, Ray, a shade-tree mechanic, figured that either the ignition switch or the starter solenoid was likely the problem.

The solenoid connects the battery to the starter motor when the key is turned to the Start position. By shorting across the solenoid terminals with a screwdriver, power goes directly to the starter motor without using the key.

Ralph's Class A had plenty of ground clearance so Ray slid halfway under it with his screwdriver to do the shorting. It worked! The engine started immediately—but the motorhome also started to move backward with the front wheel headed straight toward the middle of Ray. In Ray's own words, "I was trying to scoot sideways to the rear faster than the tire was rolling toward me, but I was losing the race and about to be turned into a wheel chock when the rig abruptly stopped." Luckily, Ralph was sitting in the driver's seat and put on the brakes.

The engine would not turn over because Ralph had left the gearshift in Reverse when he turned off the engine. This feature prevents starting the engine while in gear. Neither Ray nor Ralph had thought to check that first, which they agreed was "pretty dumb." Not having the emergency brake on when someone was underneath trying to start the engine was "pretty dumber."!

12. MR. SPARKY

Dick had stored his motorhome over the winter with the leveling jacks in the "Down" position. Come spring, he and his wife were all packed and ready to hit the road for a weekend of camping. When it became time to raise the jacks, he pushed the "Retract" button but nothing happened. After pushing the button about a dozen times, Dick decided to increase the fuse amperage from 15 to 30 amps. "Maybe a heavier fuse would make a better connection," he thought.

This time when he pressed the button, he saw sparks and heard a loud **ZZAPP**! The circuit board had multiple burned-out components but the jacks were still down.

Instead of camping, Dick used the weekend to track down a new circuit board and talk to an RV mechanic about his jack problem. The mechanic diagnosed it as most likely faulty solenoids. Sure enough, replacing the jack solenoids and the new circuit board (with a 15-amp fuse) resulted in the jacks retracting.

> **Helpful hint:** Always use the proper size fuse in electrical appliances. Oversized fuses can potentially result in blown circuit boards and electrical fires.

11. FILL 'ER UP

When Fred decided to give up RVing, he sold his diesel pusher to a man who had described himself as a long-haul trucker. Following the transaction, he spent a couple of hours going through all the systems. A few days later, Fred got a call from the buyer who said the coach had stalled. After some discussion, the reason became painfully clear: The buyer had put gasoline instead of diesel fuel in the fuel tank. Perhaps he got distracted at the fuel pump at exactly the wrong time?

Fred didn't know the extent of damages, and he certainly didn't think it was necessary to tell a trucker to put diesel in the fuel tank. Diesel fuel, unlike gasoline, acts as a lubricant for the fuel-injection system. Running a diesel engine on gasoline will cause the fuel pump to overheat and damage the fuel-injection system.

Surprisingly, no standard exists for the colors of pump handles at fuel stations to differentiate between gasoline and diesel. However, diesel handles are usually green, yellow, or black.

> **Helpful hint:** If your engine is diesel, your fuel cap should be labeled "DIESEL" as a reminder to check the pump before adding fuel.

DUMBEST THINGS

Larry MacDonald, Ph.D.

10. WHAT'S A DIPSTICK

Frank bought a used Class A motorhome and drove it for thousands of miles without a problem. One day while cruising along, an acrid smell preceded a loud **KABOOM** and immediate loss of power. The engine would not turn over.

Frank called for a tow to the nearest garage where the mechanic diagnosed a seized engine, likely caused by overheating due to lack of oil. Oil? Frank wasn't sure the last time he or anyone else had checked the oil. A potentially fine camping trip ended with he and his family renting a car and returning home until a rebuilt engine could be installed. Frank still drives his motorhome, but now he checks and changes the oil regularly.

9. A BATTERED TOAD

After a year of camping in his new motorhome without a tow car, Bert decided it was time to get a toad. He had a tow bar installed on his motorhome and purchased a brand-new vehicle. His first trip was from the dealer to a campground about 100 miles away. When he arrived at the campground, the car "smelled funny" and wouldn't start. He called the dealer to complain, and he arranged to have a local mechanic come to the campsite and check it out.

As it turned out, Bert had towed the car in gear, damaging both the engine and automatic transmission beyond repair. The dealer agreed to cover half the cost of repairs.

A few months later, Bert towed the car with the emergency brake on, resulting in severe damage to both back brakes, which had to be completely replaced because the heat had melted everything. Bert now has a waterproof Departure Checklist attached to his tow bar: Gearshift in Neutral. Brake off.

Helpful hint: Where you attach the Checklist for a towed vehicle (on the tow bar or on the driver's visor) is less important than actually looking at it before you move the rig.

8. ALMOST CLEARING CUSTOMS

Gerry and Judie were crossing the border from Canada into the U.S. in their brand-new 42' Class A. Although six lanes are normally available at Customs, congested traffic prompted Gerry to enter Lane 6. When Gerry got to the booth, the Customs Officer asked if they had any fruits or vegetables. Judie said they had a tomato, to which the officer replied, "Pull over to the right, park, and get out of your vehicle during our search." Gerry pulled forward as far as he could until a low concrete barrier required him to turn sharply right. Partway through the turn, he heard a loud **BANG**, followed by some serious crunching sounds.

An iron pole holding up the roof of the customs booth had ripped off the awning and slide topper, bent a slide, and made numerous holes and dents in the side of their motorhome. Several Customs Officers helped them pick up the pieces, apologizing profusely. Subsequent to searching their coach and confiscating the offending tomato, the Officer mentioned, "That happens almost every day."

After spending the next six weeks in an RV dealer's lot, their "beautiful baby" was repaired like new, to the tune of $15,000. In hindsight, Gerry admitted it was "driver error." He said he should have asked Judie to watch from the outside so he could have used every inch up front before turning and then watch the side so he didn't hit anything. But he didn't want to upset the Customs Officer by taking longer than necessary to get to the inspection area.

The saddest part of this story is the Officer's comment that these accidents happen almost every day (in Lane 6, apparently, since other lanes have more turning room). How difficult would it be to put a sign above Lane 6 reading "NO RVs"?

> **Helpful hint:** Most border crossings have very narrow lanes so drivers of large rigs should use extreme caution, especially with side mirrors extended. And don't even think of taking a tomato across the border!

7. DOUBLE DUMB

Grant and Doreen pulled their Class A into a gas station to fill up on their way to a nearby campground. When leaving, Grant moved ahead and while turning sharply heard a terrible grinding and ripping noise from behind their coach. Immediately stopping and getting out, they saw that their dolly fender was crumbled and the tire torn to shreds, caused by colliding with the raised concrete island at the pump. After backing the car off the dolly, Doreen drove behind the damaged dolly to the campground. Grant put their spare tire on the dolly to drive home, where they had everything repaired at a body shop.

Talk about learning from experience: The very next time they were headed to that campground, Grant decided to get fuel at the same station. When they were ready to leave, Doreen reminded him of the previous disaster. "I remember," he said, but as he pulled out, guess what? Again, the dolly hit the raised concrete island with the same damages. Now how dumb is that? Well, in my opinion, it qualified for a Dumbest Award.

I asked Doreen if they planned to get fuel at that station in the future. She replied, "Yes, but only when the dolly is safely at the campground."

6. THE NOSE KNOWS

Louie took delivery of a brand-new motorhome, driving it from the dealership to his home. The next weekend he drove to a nearby campground with his family. When he stopped at the check-in, he got a faint whiff of gasoline, but since the coach had been running smoothly, he didn't think much of it. Upon returning home at the end of the weekend, he again smelled gasoline when he got out. So, he booked an appointment at the dealership to have it checked out.

A week later cruising down the freeway on his way to the dealership with Mannheim Steamroller blaring from the CD player, Louie said he felt like he was "in absolute Heaven." Exiting the freeway, however, he smelled smoke and thought that someone was having a backyard BBQ—until he realized that the smoke was inside the coach. Pulling over to the side of the nearest street, he managed to exit just as the coach filled with smoke. A policeman stopped him from re-entering to get the fire extinguisher, saying, "The insurance company owns it now."

An investigation showed that a bracket holding the fuel line had broken, allowing gasoline to be sprayed across the hot engine. All the fire department could do was put out the flames of a charred hulk. Louie has since replaced the motorhome and his beloved Mannheim Steamroller CD, and he continues to spend many a camping trip in absolute Heaven.

Helpful hint: If you smell gasoline or diesel fuel, do not drive the vehicle until the problem is identified and repaired.

5. PRO-PAIN

Jack and Sylvia had spent a few weeks camping in their new Class A. They had worked out a division of duties such that Jack looked after the outside while Sylvia took care of the inside. One evening Jack fired up the BBQ and grilled some steaks. After they were done, he decided to leave the BBQ on for about ten minutes to burn the steak juices off the grill. On this particular evening, the Academy Awards show was just beginning on TV, which they watched while enjoying their evening meal with a glass or two of wine. After doing up the dishes, it was pretty much time to go to bed. Little did Jack know he was working on an Award of his own!

The next morning, Sylvia tried to heat up some coffee, but the stove burners wouldn't light. Jack checked the propane meter and sure enough, it was on "Empty," and, wouldn't you know it, the BBQ switch was still turned on. After minimizing his error by saying, "The tank was most likely near empty, anyway," Jack decided to drive the motorhome to a propane station across the street.

Jack did the outside departure duties while Sylvia secured the inside. With both of them seated inside, Jack drove slowly out of their site toward the exit. The sound of **KABOOM** and the motorhome coming to a grinding stop indicated that something was amiss. Their awning, still extended, had hit the first tree and was bent at a rakish angle backward. When I asked Jack why he hadn't retracted it, he said, "It was so high up that I never saw it during my walkaround." With the assistance of some helpful RVers, he managed to get it rolled back in and tied to the side as best he could. His insurance covered all but $1,800 for the awning.

Jack is one of many RVers who empty their propane tank by forgetting to turn it off, something that can easily be avoided by setting a timer or purchasing an automatic shut-off valve from a local BBQ store. Driving off with the awning extended could also be avoided by using either a Checklist or a spotter outside to watch for obstacles until the rig is clear of the site. Sylvia has since added this "Outside" duty to her inside Departure Checklist. In this case, it's obvious the propane error did not lead directly to the awning error, but two blunders in two days earned Jack a Dumbest Award.

With today's technology, wouldn't it be nice if alarm bells went off whenever the shift lever is moved from Park, indicating an extended awning, antenna, or lowered jacks? Of course, that would mean fewer Oopsies, but hey, that's what this book is all about--fewer Oopsies means more enjoyable outings in our RVs.

4. WATER FALLS

While at a campground in his smallish travel trailer, Andy's kitchen faucet stopped flowing. In the process of trying to diagnose the problem, an impromptu group excursion came up with some camping buddies, and Andy decided to go along. When he got back and opened the door, a flood of water came cascading out. His dog was standing on the dinette table, no doubt thankful he didn't have to doggy paddle until his rescue. Andy had left the faucet open. It never occurred to him to take the stopper out of the single-basin sink, "since there was no water flowing."

Andy shut off the tap at the campground hookup and mopped up the water; then left to "blow off some steam" with his buddies. Another friend, who saw Andy turn off the outside tap, thought he would be helpful by turning it back on. Several hours later, Andy returned and opened the door to another cascade of water! He had again left the faucet open with the stopper still in the sink, "since there was no water flowing!"

Apparently, a piece of plastic had become lodged in the faucet shutting off the water. For some unknown reason it shifted, allowing water to resume flowing. Andy said, "I will never ever leave the stopper in my sink again, except to do the dishes." Two floods in one day, with a little help from a friend, definitely warranted a Dumbest Award.

3. ONE COOL TRIP

As I mentioned in the Introduction, Sandy and I traveled across Canada in our RV, taking two complete summers to do so. In early October of our first year, we headed south to Florida for the winter, returning in the spring to continue our journey. This totally delightful experience sold us on the virtues of full-time RVing. Readers planning a similar trip might want to refer to my e-book, *Elly's Odyssey: Reflections on Canada*, available online. Obviously, the winners of the next Dumbest Award hadn't read my book.

Roy and his wife, Joanne, had recently retired and decided to pursue the RV lifestyle by purchasing a large motorhome. Their first major adventure would be to travel across Canada, beginning in May, from British Columbia to Newfoundland. A complete lack of pre-trip planning resulted in a number of problems, five to be exact.

Their first problem was not towing a vehicle. Very early in their trip, they discovered that "seeing the sights, especially within cities, meant taking long walks or busses and cabs after parking the motorhome some distance away."

By mid-October, they had arrived in Ontario, where they encountered their second problem. Because of occasional below-freezing temperatures, most campgrounds had already closed for the winter so they found themselves staying overnight in various parking lots. Fortunately, their furnace kept them reasonably warm.

Their third problem, related to the closed campgrounds, was dumping their black- and gray-water tanks and filling their freshwater tank. Joanne said, "Instead of seeing the sights, we spent hours trying to find a dump station and freshwater outlet."

Quite unexpectedly, they encountered their fourth problem in the province of Prince Edward Island (PEI), which Roy described as "a bunch of small towns all boarded up." Many businesses in PEI thrive on tourism and close for the winter. The same holds true for New Brunswick and Nova Scotia.

Their fifth and biggest problem occurred when Roy and Joanne had to fly back to British Columbia for a few weeks, putting their motorhome in temporary outdoor storage. When they returned, they discovered the freshwater tank had frozen solid and split open. The water lines had also broken, costing over $3,000 for repairs. Roy forked out additional money for three days in a motel while the repairs were being completed. They headed south the very next day, buying a tow car at their first opportunity.

All things considered, this was an expensive, frustrating, and eye-opening experience for these newbie RVers, one that could have easily been avoided with adequate planning.

Helpful hint: When planning an extended RV trip, do some research on your intended campgrounds and local weather conditions, especially for a cool trip! And, if you're driving a large motorhome, don't forget your tow car!

2. KEEP YOUR HEAD DOWN

Dennis was on one of his annual trips south in his Class A. This time, he had decided to take some unfamiliar back roads and had started down a grade that became rather steep. As his speed increased, he looked ahead and saw to his amazement a low-clearance bridge. His first thought was that he might get stuck under the bridge and stop traffic. "In a moment of panic," he said, "I decided to floor it."

Imagine for a moment the sound of a locomotive driving on top of your motorhome! That's what Dennis heard as steel bridge girders ripped off two air conditioners, five vents, the shower skylight, TV antenna, numerous trusses, and pieces of plywood and rubber roofing. When he finally stopped and walked back to the bridge, half his roof was strewn about the road. Dennis confirmed, "Oh, yeah, I did stop traffic," and "Oh, yeah, it was costly."

Helpful hint: New GPS models designed for RVs allow drivers to program in the height of their rigs, thus providing advance warning of low-clearance situations. Get one if you're planning to travel unfamiliar back roads.

Drumroll please ... what we've all been waiting for! Arguably, the absolutely dumbest thing reported to me over the past ten years.

1. SLIDES TRAVEL BEST WHEN RETRACTED

Barry and his wife Joan were returning home in their Class A from an enjoyable camping trip with their grandchildren. They took a toll-road exit and pulled into a restaurant parking lot for lunch. While everyone was inside the restaurant, Joan decided to get something out of the coach and had to open the bedroom slide. After lunch, Barry drove out of the parking lot onto the onramp of the toll-road and approached the tollbooth. **CRUNCH!**

The coach stopped abruptly when the still-extended slide smashed into the booth. To his dismay, Barry hadn't once looked into his rear-view mirror until that fateful moment. He also hadn't done a walkaround before moving the coach. Although drivable, the motorhome had such extensive damage that their insurance company wrote it off. The tollbooth was also totaled. Barry said that he was "a wreck for the next several days."

You might like to know that Barry and Joan are still together, bought another coach, and continue to enjoy camping with their grandchildren. They also have a strict rule about making sure slides are closed before getting underway!

Helpful hint: Always do a walk around before starting out on a trip, and again whenever your rig has been left unattended for any length of time. It only takes a minute and can save big bucks in repair bills ... just ask Barry!

Several other RVers have confessed to driving with a slide extended, mostly without incident. However, one man did report getting his bedroom slide caught on a telephone-pole guy wire, causing extensive damage to the slide awning.

It surprises me that motorhome manufacturers allow the rig to move when a slide is extended. Some coaches may have warning lights on the dashboard, but if drivers don't look in their rear-view mirror, why would they look at their dashboard?

Larry MacDonald, Ph.D.

GENERAL OBSERVATIONS ABOUT RV MISHAPS

By far, the most common mishap that RVers report is hitting things while backing up, usually without a spotter.

The second most frequent mishap is a toss-up between blackwater and tow-car issues.

Once you've done something dumb, it's not likely you'll repeat it (with the odd exceptions, such as Numbers 7 and 4 in this book).

Experience is *not* the best teacher when it comes to RV mishaps. Knowledge of someone else's mishap is the best teacher. Why? Because it's so much cheaper!

Sickening sounds, such as **CRUNCH** and **KABOOM**, are often associated with the unexpected and mostly avoidable costs of RVing.

The main causes of RV mishaps are rushing through things, becoming impatient, getting distracted, and multi-tasking (thinking or doing more than one thing at a time). Alcohol sometimes plays a role as well!

It's no coincidence that Dumber and Dumbest Things are more traumatic and costly than your run-of-the-mill Dumb Things.

Of all the RV mishaps reported to me, 90% were caused by males, 9% by females, and 1% by animals. Yes, animals! One locked his owners out of their motorhome; the other was blocking the passenger-side mirror while the owner was backing into a post. Both were large dogs—probably males!

Arrival and Departure Checklists (see Appendix) can prevent many mishaps (about a third of those reported), but only if you use them!

Larry MacDonald, Ph.D.

APPENDIX

I made up the following Checklists for a friend who just started RVing in a Class C motorhome. Feel free to modify as necessary to suit your type of rig. They can also be found on my website: www.LandYachting.ca.

Arrival Checklist

Check In

- ☐ Park near office where indicated by signs "Check-in Parking"

- ☐ Ask if a discount is offered, such as Good Sam or Passport America

- ☐ Request a map of the campground and ask for best route to your site

- ☐ Ask if site is full service (power, water, sewer)

- ☐ Request information on park facilities of interest, including entry codes

- ☐ Ask about local attractions, such as tours, restaurants, hiking trails, etc.

- ☐ Ask if Wi-Fi is offered and whether a password is required

- ☐ Ask if cable TV is available at site (some campgrounds have cable boxes)

Locating RV Site

- [ ] Find your site on map and determine best entry and exit paths

- [ ] If site has no sewer, drive to dump station and empty tanks, if needed

- [ ] If site has no water, drive to available faucet and fill tank, if needed

- [ ] Drive to site, watching for tight turns and low trees along the way

- [ ] BEFORE entering site, check for obstacles (picnic table, trees, fire pits, posts)

- [ ] Confirm site has facilities (power, water, sewer) and test water faucet

- [ ] Unhitch tow-car unless site is pull-through

Driving in and Parking

- [ ] Drive into site, USING SPOTTER, in reach of facilities

- [ ] Ensure slide can be opened without obstructions

- [ ] Level RV, using leveling blocks under tires if necessary

- [ ] Set emergency brake on RV and tow car; and lock car

Setting Up

- ☐ If you have an RV surge protector, plug it into electrical outlet and check power

- ☐ Turn OFF switch at panel, plug in cord to RV, then to panel; turn ON switch

- ☐ Open slide, making sure there are no obstructions inside OR outside

- ☐ Attach water-pressure regulator at tap; connect hose and water filter

- ☐ Connect sewer line; making sure blackwater valve is closed

- ☐ Open gray tank, unless you want to save water to flush out sewer hose before leaving

- ☐ Turn fridge over to Electric and turn ON hot-water heater

- ☐ Plug in TV cable or raise roof antenna

That's it! Pour a glass of wine and relax ...

Departure Checklist

Interior

- ☐ Store loose items
- ☐ Close cupboards
- ☐ Secure drawers
- ☐ Close ceiling vents
- ☐ Lower TV antenna
- ☐ Secure refrigerator and switch to propane
- ☐ Check level in freshwater tank; add water if required upon departure
- ☐ Close windows and lower blinds
- ☐ Bring slide in BEFORE removing power cable
- ☐ Turn OFF water heater, furnace, water pump, and lights
- ☐ Place trash and recyclable items in campground bins

Exterior

- ☐ Drain holding tanks … black water first; then gray water. Close blackwater valve.
- ☐ Then add chemicals and 2 gallons of water to black tank through toilet
- ☐ Disconnect power cable, water hoses, sewer line, and TV cable

- ☐ Switch water manifold on NORMAL

- ☐ Retract awning

- ☐ Close and lock entry door and outside storage cabinets

- ☐ Stow entry steps

- ☐ Retract stabilizer jacks

Before Departure

- ☐ Conduct safety inspection – check turn signals, lights, tires, and rear-view camera, clean windows and adjust mirrors

- ☐ Walk around RV checking windows, slide, TV antenna, vents, cables, tires, jacks, and entry steps

- ☐ Walk around tow car checking hitch, turn signals, brake lights, tires, steering unlocked, emergency brake OFF, gearshift in Neutral

- ☐ Watch for tail swing when turning out of campsite

- ☐ Check for items left in campsite (water-pressure regulator, door mat, leveling blocks, clotheslines, spouse)

- ☐ Program next destination on GPS and confirm suggested route on roadmap BEFORE leaving campground

That's it! You're on your way to a new adventure … safe travels!

Larry MacDonald, Ph.D.

About the Author

Larry MacDonald is a freelance journalist from British Columbia, Canada. Together with his wife, Sandy, and their pets, he has been RVing in motorhomes and fifth-wheel trailers for over 30 years in the US, Canada, and even once in New Zealand.

Ten years ago, their first major RV trip resulted in an e-book, *Elly's Odyssey: Reflections on Canada,* that describes their journey across Canada with their dog, Elly. They have been full-timing ever since and loving every minute—well, except for those occasions where Larry did some dumb things (described in the Introduction)! Their current rig is a 38-foot Big Sky Montana fifth-wheel trailer.

Larry's Ph.D. in Experimental Psychology, a keen interest in teaching, and a wry sense of humor provide a unique set of attributes that are evident throughout *RV Oopsies*. He has published articles about RVing in various magazines, including *MotorHome, Trailer Life, and Canadian RVing*, some of which can be found on his website: www.LandYachting.ca. Prior careers included Psychologist, Professor, Researcher, Administrator, and Entrepreneur. Since retiring, he mostly enjoys life on the road, learning and writing about people, places, and the dumb things that RVers do.

www.ingramcontent.com/pod-product-compliance
Lightning Source LLC
Chambersburg PA
CBHW041139170426
43199CB00023B/2925